UNDERSTANDING
RETURN
ON
INVESTMENT

Other related books include:

Understanding Income Statements by Franklin J. Plewa, Jr., and George T. Friedlob

Understanding Cash Flow by Franklin J. Plewa, Jr., and George T. Friedlob

Understanding Balance Sheets by George T. Friedlob and Franklin J. Plewa, Jr.

How to Read a Financial Report by John A. Tracy

UNDERSTANDING RETURN ON INVESTMENT

George T. Friedlob
Franklin J. Plewa, Jr.

JOHN WILEY & SONS, INC.
New York • Chichester • Brisbane • Toronto • Singapore

We gratefully acknowledge the patience and understanding of our families and dedicate this work to them.

Preface

*T*he most common measure of profitability and management performance is return on investment (ROI). ROI is often thought to be a better measure of profit performance than profit itself because ROI considers the investment base required to generate profit.

The primary objectives of this book are to:

1. Explain the meaning of ROI and its components.
2. Describe the use of ROI to evaluate both external and internal operations.
3. Provide a working discussion of the various forms of ROI and how they provide different measures for evaluating investment activities.
4. Introduce the methods most often used by managers to analyze and control revenues and costs.
5. Demonstrate how maximizing ROI impacts the choice of managerial tools used to make long-term business decisions.

Chapters 1 and 2 introduce the concept of ROI and the DuPont system of financial analysis. Chapter 3 discusses the relationship of ROI to another important performance index, return on equity (ROE). The problems associated with using or being evaluated by ROI are examined in Chapter 4, and the effect of ROI on investment and disinvestment decisions is discussed in Chapter 5.

Chapter 6 looks at the options available to determine profit and the investment base used to calculate ROI. Chapter 7 discusses how to value the investment base. Chapters 8, 9, and 10 present three little-known but very useful measures of ROI—gross margin ROI, contribution margin ROI, and cash ROI. How managers analyze sales revenues and costs is covered in Chapters 11 and 12.

Chapter 13 explains how ROI is used to evaluate investment centers in a decentralized operation, and Chapter 14 describes the problems and benefits of using transfer prices to control costs and improve management performance. The weighted average cost of capital and its use in making investment decisions is covered in Chapter 15.

Chapter 16 explains how to calculate the time value of money, a technical concept required for an understanding of the discounted cash flow methods used to evaluate capital investments—the topic of Chapter 18. Chapter 17 explains how companies forecast cash returns and use the depreciation tax shield to improve cash inflow. Chapters 19 and 20 discuss and compare nondiscounted cash flow methods used in capital budgeting decisions. Finally, Chapter 21 presents important ratios that interact with ROI.

Our intention is to create a working reference that helps you understand how ROI is used to measure company performance and evaluate managers. We hope this information helps you make good management decisions—and lots of money!

GEORGE T. FRIEDLOB
FRANKLIN J. PLEWA, JR.

Clemson, South Carolina
Pocatello, Idaho
March 1996

Contents

Contents

UNDERSTANDING
RETURN
ON
INVESTMENT

1

THE IMPORTANCE
OF RETURN
ON INVESTMENT

Owners create a company to increase their own wealth. Thus, owners are seeking profitability in all phases of operations. Creditors are concerned about whether the company is using its resources profitably so it can pay interest and principal on its debt. Company managers must show they can manage the owners' investment and produce the profits owners and creditors demand. Because top management must meet the profit expectations of company owners, profitability goals are passed down from top management to lower levels of management and then spread throughout the company. The end result is that all managers are charged with profitability goals, which are often increased and tightened as each level of management seeks a margin of safety (see Exhibit 1–1).

How is profitability measured and how are standards determined? Is it enough for managers to report that earnings for the year are some amount—say, $500,000? Earnings are determined by subtracting a company's business expenses—salaries, interest payments, and cost of goods sold, for example—from the revenues it realizes from sales, investments, and other sources.

Suppose a company income statement is composed of the following.

Hypothetical Company

Income Statement

for the Year Ended December 31, 1996

Sales	$20,000,000
Expenses	19,500,000
Profit	$ 500,000

EXHIBIT 1–1
Profit Goals May Increase as They Are Delegated

☺	Board Chair	"Let's target 5 percent profit."
☺	President	"We need 10 percent profit this year."
😐	Vice President	"Your goal is 15 percent."
☹	Middle Manager	"We've got to turn a 20 percent profit!"
😠	Line Manager	"Earn 25 percent or else!"

Does this income statement indicate that company managers have performed well? Probably not; with sales activity of $20,000,000, the owners, creditors, and top management would expect a higher profit: $500,000 is only 2.5 percent of $20,000,000. We give this verdict on management's performance because of the intuitive expectation that profit must be linked to activity if one is to assess the adequacy of a company's profit or evaluate the efforts of a company's management.

Suppose, instead, that our hypothetical company had the following income statement.

Hypothetical Company
Income Statement
for the Year Ended December 31, 1996

Sales	$3,125,000
Expenses	2,625,000
Profit	$ 500,000

4

We can see a stronger relationship between profit and activity when $500,000 profit is generated by sales of $3,125,000. Profit is now 16.0 percent of sales.

Still, to draw correct conclusions about the adequacy of profit, we need to know more than the absolute dollar amount of profit ($500,000) and the relationship between profit and activity (16.0 percent in our example). Suppose the second income statement, with sales of $3,125,000 and profit of $500,000, was generated by a management team that ran a company with assets—plant, equipment, inventories, and other items—that totaled $25,000,000. Does this new information change our opinion of the performance of the management team? The calculation would be:

$$\text{ROI} = \frac{\text{Profit}}{\text{Investment}}$$

$$\text{ROI} = \frac{\$500,000}{\$25,000,000}$$

$$\text{ROI} = 0.02 \text{ or } 2.0\%$$

A 2.0 percent return on an investment of $25,000,000 is not acceptable! The owners would be better off with their funds invested in U.S. Treasury bills (T-bills) or a savings account: the return would be better, and there would be no risk. A company must generate a much higher return than T-bills or savings accounts to justify the risk involved in doing business.

Suppose that the $500,000 profit was earned with only $2,000,000 invested in assets, rather than $25,000,000.

$$\text{ROI} = \frac{\text{Profit}}{\text{Investment}}$$

$$\text{ROI} = \frac{\$500,000}{\$2,000,000}$$

$$\text{ROI} = 0.25 \text{ or } 25.0\%$$

ROI is now 25.0 percent, a much higher return than the ROI one expects from T-bills, government bonds, or bank savings accounts.

This rate of return is much more acceptable to owners and creditors than the 2.0 percent return.

The relationship between profit and the investment that generates profit is one of the most widely used measures of company performance. As a quantitative measure of investment and results, ROI provides a company's management with a simple tool for examining performance. By determining ROI, management can reduce the factors of intuition and judgment to an interpretable mathematical calculation and compare alternative uses of invested capital (for example, "Should we increase inventory or pay off some of our debt?").

Creditors and owners can always invest in government securities, which yield a low rate of return but are essentially risk free. Riskier investments require higher rates of return (reward) to attract potential investors. ROI relates profit (the reward) to the size of the investment used to generate it.

Uses of ROI

Profit is generally created only when a company operates effectively. Management's operating effectiveness is proven if the company can prosper, obtain funding, and reward the suppliers of its funds. ROI is the principal tool used to evaluate how well (or poorly) management performs.

Creditors and Owners

ROI is used by creditors and owners to:

1. *Assess the company's ability to earn an adequate rate of return.*
   Creditors and owners can compare the ROI of a company to those of other companies and to industry benchmarks or norms. ROI provides information about a company's financial health.

2. ***Provide information about the effectiveness of management.*** Tracking ROI over a period of time assists in determining whether a company has capable management.

3. ***Project future earnings.*** Potential suppliers of capital assess present and future investment and the return expected from that investment.

Managers

ROI is more than a device to assess company performance. ROI is also a tool used by managers at different levels who must choose among alternatives to maximize profit and add value to the company. Managers use ROI to:

1. ***Measure the performance of individual company segments when each segment is treated as an investment center.*** In an investment center, each segment manager controls both profit and an investment base. ROI is the basic tool used to assess both profitability and performance.

2. ***Evaluate capital expenditure proposals.*** Capital budgeting is long-term planning for such items as renewal, replacement, or expansion of plant facilities. Most capital budgeting decisions rely heavily on discounted cash flow techniques.

3. ***Assist in setting management goals.*** Budgeting quantifies a manager's plans. Most effective approaches to goal setting use a participative budgeting process: each manager participates in setting goals and standards and in establishing operating budgets that meet those goals and standards. Most budgeting efforts begin or end with a target ROI.

Perhaps the biggest reason for the popularity of ROI is its simplicity. A company's ROI is directly comparable to returns on other, perhaps more familiar investments (such as a savings account at a bank) and to the company's cost of capital. If a company pays 10 percent interest on capital but earns only 8 percent, that's bad. If it pays 10 percent interest on capital but earns 15 percent, that's good. What could be simpler?

Alone or in combination with other measures, ROI is the most commonly used management indicator of company profit and performance. ROI is a comprehensive tool that normalizes dissimilar activities of different sizes, and allows them to be compared. ROI has its faults and its advantages. It is sometimes ticklish to use if you don't understand it completely.

That's what we believe we tell you in this book.

2

ROI AND THE DuPONT SYSTEM OF FINANCIAL ANALYSIS

Many senior managers find ROI useful because it is an overall measure, affected by a manager's activity in many different areas. Consider, for example, managers of two companies that have each earned income of $10,000, on an investment of $100,000, to produce ROIs of 10 percent.

$$\text{Company One ROI} = \frac{\$10,000}{\$100,000} = 0.10$$

$$\text{Company Two ROI} = \frac{\$10,000}{\$100,000} = 0.10$$

The two managers produced the same ROI, but are their business activities otherwise the same? Might these managers have arrived at the same ROI by using completely different strategies?

To illustrate, let us imagine that both companies are retail jewelers. Company One sells inexpensive costume jewelry in malls throughout the country and follows a high-volume, low-markup approach to marketing. Thus, the profit margin on Company One's $500,000 of sales is only 2 percent, calculated as follows.

$$\text{Profit margin on sales} = \frac{\text{Profit}}{\text{Sales}}$$

$$\text{Profit margin on sales} = \frac{\$10,000}{\$500,000} = 0.02$$

Likewise, Company One's assets turn over rapidly. Although asset turnover is a somewhat intuitive concept, analysts calculate turnover by dividing an asset into the best measure of the asset's activity. Sales is the best measure of the activity of total assets. If Company One creates sales of $500,000 with its investment of $100,000, its asset turnover is 5 times per year, calculated as follows.

$$\text{Company One investment turnover} = \frac{\text{Sales}}{\text{Investment}}$$

$$\text{Company One investment turnover} = \frac{\$500,000}{\$100,000} = 5 \text{ times}$$

Notice that the ROI generated is the product of Company One's investment turnover and its profit margin on sales. The investment turnover is a measure of how active Company One has been. The profit margin on sales is a measure of how profitable that activity has been. Because Company One is very active, the profit margin on each sale can be low.

$$\frac{\text{Investment}}{\text{turnover}} \times \frac{\text{Profit margin}}{\text{on sales}} = \text{ROI}$$

$$\frac{\text{Sales}}{\text{Investment}} \times \frac{\text{Profit}}{\text{Sales}} = \frac{\text{Profit}}{\text{Investment}}$$

$$\frac{\$500,000}{\$100,000} \times \frac{\$10,000}{\$500,000} = \frac{\$10,000}{\$100,000} = 0.10$$

$$\text{ROI} = 5 \text{ times} \times 0.02 = 0.10$$

Company Two does not operate like Company One. Company Two's $125,000 of sales were of expensive, one-of-a-kind jewelry containing large diamonds and other precious stones. Because each piece is unique, Company Two has low asset activity (turnover) and sells only a small volume of jewelry, but with high profit on each sale. As a result, Company Two turns its assets only 1.25 times per year.

$$\text{Investment turnover} = \frac{\text{Sales}}{\text{Investment}}$$

$$\text{Investment turnover} = \frac{\$125,000}{\$100,000} = 1.25 \text{ times}$$

Because the investment turnover for Company Two is lower than that of Company One, Company Two must demand a higher profit margin on its sales, compared to Company One, if it is to generate the same ROI. The profit margin on sales for Company Two is 8 percent. With this markup, Company Two matches Company One in achieving an ROI of 10 percent, but by a different combination of turnover (activity) and margin (profitability).

$$\text{Investment turnover} \times \text{Profit margin on sales} = \text{ROI}$$

Company One 5 times ×	0.02	= 0.10
Company Two 1.25 times ×	0.08	= 0.10

Managers who wish to increase their ROI must realize that it is the result of these two factors, activity and margin. For instance, could the manager of Company One increase ROI if turnover of assets increased to 5.5 times per year as a result of lowering the profit margin on sales to 1.5 percent?

$$5.5 \text{ times} \times 0.015 = 0.0825$$

No; that will not work. ROI would decrease to 8.25 percent. However, using the following two steps, the manager can calculate the profit margin necessary to increase ROI to a targeted 11 percent with a turnover of 5.5 times per year.

$$\text{Investment turnover} \times \text{Profit margin} = \text{Targeted ROI}$$

$$5.5 \qquad \times \qquad ? \qquad = \qquad 0.11$$

$$\frac{\text{Targeted ROI}}{\text{Investment turnover}} = \text{Profit margin}$$

$$\frac{0.11}{5.5} = 0.02$$

The manager must turn assets 5.5 times with a 0.02 profit margin on sales, in order to generate an 11 percent ROI.

MCI and RJR Nabisco

Financial reports of companies in different industries demonstrate the phenomenon of equivalent ROI arrived at by using different strategies. MCI Communications and RJR Nabisco had nearly the same ROIs in 1994. The income statements and balance sheets of these two companies are shown in Exhibits 2–1 and 2–2, respectively. Their ROIs are calculated below, using net operating income as the return. Operating income is a company's income from its regular business activities. Operating income is thought to be a better measure of the earnings a company can continue to realize, year after year, as compared to net income, which is affected by unusual gains and losses or by changes in debt and interest expense.

$$\frac{\text{Profit (net operating income)}}{\text{Investment}} = \text{ROI}$$

$$\text{MCI } \frac{\$1,456}{\$16,366} = 0.089$$

$$\text{RJR Nabisco } \frac{\$2,550}{\$31,408} = 0.081$$

How did these two companies create these returns? What strategies did their managers take? When we separate the ROIs into their investment turnover and profit margin components, we see that RJR Nabisco's asset turnover is more than four times that of MCI, and that MCI's profit margin on sales is almost five times that of RJR Nabisco. RJR Nabisco followed a strategy of more active asset use; MCI had more profitable sales. (The details of these calculations are in Exhibit 2–3.)

Investment turnover		× Profit margin	= ROI
MCI 0.109 times	×	0.815	= 0.089
RJR Nabisco 0.489 times	×	0.166	= 0.081

EXHIBIT 2–1
Income Statements for MCI Communications
Corporation and Subsidiaries

Year ended December 31,	1994	1993	1992
(In millions, except per share amounts)			
Revenue	$13,338	$11,921	$10,562
Operating expenses			
Telecommunications	6,916	6,373	5,684
Sales, operations and general	3,790	3,310	2,794
Depreciation	1,176	970	873
Total operating expenses	11,882	10,653	9,351
Income from operations	1,456	1,268	1,211
Interest expense	(153)	(178)	(218)
Interest income	50	8	3
Other expense, net	(73)	(53)	(33)
Income before income taxes and **extraordinary item**	1,280	1,045	963
Income tax provision	485	418	354
Income before extraordinary item	795	627	609
Extraordinary loss on early debt retirements, less applicable tax benefit of $26 million	—	45	—
Net income	$ 795	$ 582	$ 609
Dividends on preferred stock	1	1	20
Earnings applicable to common **stockholders**	$ 794	$ 581	$ 589
Earnings per common and common **equivalent shares**			
Income before extraordinary item	$ 1.32	$ 1.12	$ 1.11
Loss on early debt retirements	—	(.08)	—
Total	$ 1.32	$ 1.04	$ 1.11
Weighted average number of common shares	604	562	532

(continued)

EXHIBIT 2–1 (continued)

Balance Sheets for MCI Communications Corporation and Subsidiaries

December 31,	1994	1993
(In millions)		
Assets		
Current assets		
Cash and cash equivalents	$ 1,429	$ 165
Marketable securities	839	—
Receivables, net of allowance for uncollectibles of $226		
and $211 million	2,266	2,131
Other current assets	354	305
Total current assets	4,888	2,601
Communications system		
System in service	9,766	8,563
Other property and equipment	2,452	2,172
Total communications system in service	12,218	10,735
Accumulated depreciation	(4,349)	(4,297)
Construction in progress	1,190	883
Total communications system, net	9,059	7,321
Other assets		
Goodwill, net	1,103	1,093
Noncurrent marketable securities	824	—
Investment in affiliates	199	30
Other assets and deferred charges, net	293	231
Total other assets	2,419	1,354
Total assets	$16,366	$11,276
Liabilities and stockholders' equity		
Current liabilities		
Accrued telecommunications expense	$ 1,505	$ 1,507
Accounts payable	609	742
Other accrued liabilities	893	737
Long-term debt due within one year	130	215
Total current liabilities	3,137	3,201
Noncurrent liabilities		
Long-term debt	2,997	2,366
Deferred taxes and other	1,228	996
Total noncurrent liabilities	4,225	3,362
Stockholders' equity		
Preferred stock, $.10 par value, authorized 50 million shares and 20 million shares: Series D convertible, outstanding 0 and 13,736 shares	—	1
Class A common stock, $.10 par value, authorized 500 million and 0 shares, issued and outstanding 136 million and 0 shares	14	—
Common stock, $.10 par value, authorized 2 billion and 800 million shares, issued 592 million shares	60	60
Additional paid in capital	6,227	2,493
Retained earnings	3,548	2,785
Treasury stock at cost, 48 and 51 million shares	(845)	(626)
Total stockholders' equity	9,004	4,713
Total liabilities and stockholders' equity	$16,366	$11,276

EXHIBIT 2-2
Consolidated Statements of Income and
Retained Earnings for RJR Nabisco

($ in millions except per share amounts)	Year Ended December 31, 1994		Year Ended December 31, 1993		Year Ended December 31, 1992	
	Holdings	RJRN	Holdings	RJRN	Holdings	RJRN
Net sales (Note 1)	$ 15,366	$15,366	$ 15,104	$15,104	$ 15,734	$15,734
Costs and expenses (Note 1):						
Cost of products sold	6,977	6,977	6,640	6,640	6,326	6,326
Selling, advertising, admin istrative and general expenses	5,210	5,198	5,731	5,723	5,788	5,776
Amortization of trademarks and goodwill	629	629	625	625	616	616
Restructuring expense	—	—	730	730	106	106
Operating income	2,550	2,562	1,378	1,386	2,898	2,910
Interest and debt expense (Notes 8 and 10)	(1,065)	(1,065)	(1,209)	(1,186)	(1,449)	(1,359)
Other income (expense), net	(110)	(121)	(58)	(88)	7	(75)
Income before income taxes	1,375	1,376	111	112	1,456	1,476
Provision for income taxes (Note 3)	611	614	114	116	680	693
Income (loss) before extraordinary item	764	762	(3)	(4)	776	783
Extraordinary item—loss on early extinguishments of debt, debt net of income taxes (Note 4)	(245)	(245)	(142)	(135)	(477)	(464)
Net income (loss)	519	517	(145)	(139)	299	319
Less preferred stock dividends	131	—	68	—	31	—
Net income (loss) applicable to common stock	388	517	(213)	(139)	268	319
Retained earnings (accumulated deficit) at beginning of period	(883)	(459)	(738)	(320)	(1,037)	(639)
Dividends paid to parent and charged to retained earnings	—	(42)	—	—	—	—
Add preferred stock dividends charged to paid-in capital	131	—	68	—	31	—
Retained earnings (accumulated deficit) at end of period (Note 13)	$ (364)	$ 16	$ (883)	$ (459)	$ (738)	$ (320)
Net income (loss) per common and common equivalent share (Note 2):						
Income (loss) before extraordinary item	$ 0.41	—	$ (0.05)	—	$ 0.55	—
Extraordinary item	(0.16)	—	(0.10)	—	(0.35)	—
Net income (loss)	$ 0.25	—	$ (0.15)	—	$ 0.20	—
Pro forma net income (loss) per common and common equivalent share (Note 2)	$ 1.26	—	$ (0.79)	—	$ 0.98	—
Dividends per share of Series A Preferred Stock (Note 12)	$ 2.92	—	$ 3.34	—	$ 3.34	—
Dividends per share of Series C Preferred Stock (Note 12)	$ 3.94	—	—	—	—	—
Average number of common and common equivalent shares outstanding (in thousands) (Note 2)	$1,538,127	—	$1,349,196	—	$1,363,549	—

(continued)

EXHIBIT 2–2 (continued)
Consolidated Balance Sheets for RJR Nabisco

($ in millions)	December 31, 1994		December 31, 1993	
	Holdings	RJRN	Holdings	RJRN
Assets				
Current assets:				
Cash and cash equivalents (Note 5)	$ 423	$ 409	$ 215	$ 205
Accounts and notes receivable, net (Note 5)	934	934	856	847
Inventories (Note 6)	2,580	2,580	2,700	2,700
Prepaid expenses and excise taxes	426	426	374	374
Total current assets	4,363	4,349	4,145	4,126
Property, plant and equipment—at cost	7,767	7,767	7,166	7,166
Less accumulated depreciation	(2,333)	(2,333)	(1,998)	(1,998)
Net property, plant and equipment (Note 7)	5,434	5,434	5,168	5,168
Trademarks, net of accumulated amortization of $1,491 and $1,223, respectively	8,506	8,506	8,727	8,727
Goodwill, net of accumulated amortization of $2,124 and $1,767, respectively	12,681	12,681	12,851	12,851
Other assets and deferred charges	424	423	404	400
	$31,408	$31,393	$31,295	$31,272
Liabilities and Stockholders' Equity				
Current liabilities:				
Notes payable (Note 8)	$ 296	$ 296	$ 301	$ 301
Accounts payable	548	548	515	515
Accrued liabilities (Note 9)	2,532	2,488	2,751	2,570
Current maturities of long-term debt (Notes 10 and 17)	1,970	1,970	142	142
Income taxes accrued (Note 3)	248	248	234	234
Total current liabilities	5,594	5,550	3,943	3,897
Long-term debt (less current maturities) (Notes 10 and 17)	8,883	8,883	12,005	12,005
Other noncurrent liabilities	2,235	1,836	2,503	2,353
Deferred income taxes (Note 3)	3,788	3,714	3,774	3,701
Commitment and contingencies (Note 11)				
Stockholders' equity (Notes 12, 13 and 17):				
ESOP convertible preferred stock—15,315,130 and 15,573,973 shares issued and outstanding at December 31, 1994 and 1993, respectively	245	—	249	—
Series A convertible preferred stock—52,500,000 shares issued and outstanding at December 31, 1993	—	—	2	—
Series B preferred stock—50,000 shares issued and outstanding at December 31, 1994 and 1993	1,250	—	1,250	—
Series C preferred stock—26,675,000 shares issued and outstanding at December 31, 1994	3	—	—	—
Common stock—1,361,656,883 and 1,138,011,292 shares issued and outstanding at December 31, 1994 and 1993, respectively	13	—	11	—
Paid-in capital	10,147	11,558	8,778	9,877
Cumulative translation adjustments	(164)	(164)	(102)	(102)
Retained earnings (accumulated deficit)	(364)	16	(883)	(459)
Receivable from ESOP	(186)	—	(211)	—
Loans receivable from employees	(14)	—	(18)	—
Unamortized value of restricted stock	(22)	—	(6)	—
Total stockholders' equity	10,908	11,410	9,070	9,316
	$31,408	$31,393	$31,295	$31,272

18

EXHIBIT 2–3
Ratio Calculations for MCI and RJR Nabisco (Amounts in Millions)

Investment turnover × Profit margin = ROI

MCI	$\dfrac{\text{Sales}}{\text{Investment}}$	×	$\dfrac{\text{Profit}}{\text{Sales}}$		= ROI
	$\dfrac{\$13,338}{\$16,366}$	×	$\dfrac{\$1,456}{\$13,338}$		= 0.089
	0.109	×	0.815		= 0.089
RJR Nabisco	$\dfrac{\text{Sales}}{\text{Investment}}$	×	$\dfrac{\text{Profit}}{\text{Sales}}$		= ROI
	$\dfrac{\$15,366}{\$31,408}$	×	$\dfrac{\$2,550}{\$15,366}$		= 0.081
	0.489	×	0.166		= 0.081

RJR Nabisco Segmental ROI Analysis

RJR Nabisco did not follow the same strategy in all parts of the company because different industries demand different combinations of activity and margin. Exhibit 2–4 contains RJR Nabisco's disclosure, in the notes to its financial statements, of the performance of its tobacco and food segments. Segmental ROI, turnover, and margin ratios follow.

Investment turnover × Profit margin = ROI
Tobacco 0.395 × 0.238 = 0.094
Food 0.643 × 0.121 = 0.078

The ROI for RJR Nabisco's tobacco segment is greater than that for the company as a whole; the ROI for the food segment is lower. The tobacco segment had a profit margin twice as great as the food segment. However, this difference was in part offset by the higher asset turnover of the food segment. If the food segment could generate

EXHIBIT 2-4

RJR Nabisco's Note Disclosure of the Performance of Its Tobacco and Food Segments

	Year Ended December 31, 1994	Year Ended December 31, 1993	Year Ended December 31, 1992
Net sales:			
Tobacco	$ 7,667	$ 8,079	$ 9,027
Food	7,699	7,025	6,707
Consolidated net sales	$15,366	$15,104	$15,734
Operating income:			
Tobacco (1)(2)	$ 1,826	$ 893	$ 2,241
Food (1)(2)	931	624	769
Headquarters (2)	(207)	(139)	(112)
Consolidated operating income	$ 2,550	$ 1,378	$ 2,898
Capital expenditures:			
Tobacco	$ 215	$ 224	$ 189
Food	455	391	330
Consolidated capital expenditures	$ 670	$ 615	$ 519
Depreciation expense:			
Tobacco	$ 228	$ 237	$ 252
Food	218	207	197
Headquarters	8	4	6
Consolidated depreciation expense	$ 454	$ 448	$ 455

	December 31, 1994	December 31, 1993
Assets:		
Tobacco	$19,420	$19,904
Food	11,917	11,270
Headquarters (3)	71	121
Consolidated assets	$31,408	$31,295

(1) Includes amortization of trademarks and goodwill for Tobacco and Food, respectively, for the year ended December 31, 1994, of $404 million and $225 million; for the year ended December 31, 1993, of $407 million and $218 million and for the year ended December 31, 1992, of $404 million and $212 million.

(2) The 1993 and 1992 amounts include the effects of the restructuring expense at Tobacco (1993—$544 million; 1992—$43 million), Food (1993—$153 million; 1992—$63 million) and Headquarters (1993—$33; 1992—$0), and the 1992 gain ($98 million) from the sale of Holdings' ready-to-eat cold cereal business (See Note 1 to the Consolidated Financial Statements).

(3) Cash and cash equivalents for the domestic operating companies are included in Headquarters' assets.

the same margin as tobacco, what would its ROI be? The food segment would greatly increase its ROI if it could improve its margin to equal that of tobacco.

$$\text{Investment turnover} \quad \times \text{Profit margin} = \text{ROI}$$
$$\text{Food (with increased margin) } 0.643 \times \quad 0.238 \quad = 0.153$$

The DuPont Method

The DuPont system of financial control is an ROI-based management system that begins, as we have, by separating ROI into its turnover and margin components. Each of these components is then broken down into its own components, then into subcomponents, and so forth. For

EXHIBIT 2–5
A Formula Chart Used in the DuPont System of
Financial Management

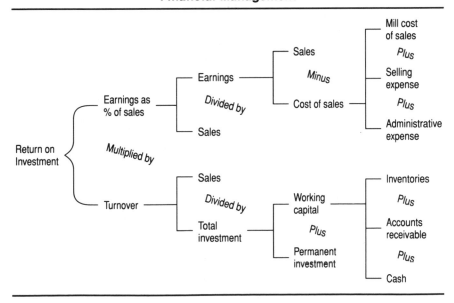

example, margin is composed of two components, profit and sales. Sales is the product of price and quantity components; profit is the result of subtracting many expenses from revenues. Exhibit 2–5 shows the best known of the formula charts used in the DuPont system to analyze or plan changes in ROI.

From Exhibit 2–5 (or other charts like it), we can see that a manager's actions, in *many* areas, directly impact ROI. For example, if cash is managed poorly, so that available balances are needlessly high, working capital and total investment will also be high. As a direct result of higher investment, turnover will be lowered and ROI decreased.

The breakdown of ROI into margin and turnover has a number of advantages in profit planning. The components are shown as equally important in improving ROI, and the importance of sales is explicitly recognized. When managers examine the formula charts used in the DuPont system of financial management, they see the multitude of trade-offs and choices available.

3

ROI AND ROE

*M*any investors are as concerned (or even more concerned) about return on equity (ROE) as they are about ROI. Equity means simply "property rights" and refers to the interests of both owners and creditors, but the "equity" in ROE is defined as "*shareholder* equity" only. Thus, ROE measures the return on shareholders' investment in the company rather than the return on the company's investment in assets. For an investor, ROE is the most important return.

ROE differs from ROI because a company typically borrows part of its capital. Consider a company that creates a 15 percent ROI.

$$ROI = \frac{Profit}{Investment}$$

$$ROI = \frac{\$90,000}{\$600,000} = 0.15$$

If all the investment in assets ($600,000) is financed by owners, then owners' equity is also $600,000 and ROE is also 15 percent.

$$ROE = \frac{Profit}{Equity} = \frac{\$90,000}{\$600,000} = 0.15$$

But if one-third of the investment in assets is borrowed, and owners' equity is only $400,000, ROE is increased to 22.5 percent. If half of the assets are from borrowed capital, ROE rises to 30 percent. At three-quarters debt, ROE is 45 percent.

$$ROE = \frac{Profit}{Equity} = \frac{\$90,000}{\$400,000} = 0.225$$

$$ROE = \frac{Profit}{Equity} = \frac{\$90,000}{\$300,000} = 0.30$$

$$ROE = \frac{Profit}{Equity} = \frac{\$90,000}{\$200,000} = 0.45$$

The proportion of assets obtained by debt financing rather than owner investment is important because debt "leverages" the owners' investment. Take the analogy of a lever placed across a fulcrum, which transfers pressure on the long end of the lever into a greatly magnified force on the short end, giving a powerful mechanical advantage. In the same sense, financial leverage gives a financial advantage, increasing ROE when companies borrow and then earn and ROI on the borrowed funds that is greater than the interest rate. Although the interest lowers earnings somewhat, the owners' investment is much smaller and the effect of earnings is magnified, increasing the ROE. Although we omit implicit consideration of interest here, increasing debt generally increases ROE.

Solvency

Ratios of debt and equity are called solvency or leverage ratios. Examples include debt to owners' equity, debt to total equities (debt plus owners' equity), and the inverse of these ratios. Debt and equity ratios determine the relative sizes of the property rights of creditors and owners. Too much debt restricts managers and increases the risk of owners, because debt increases the fixed charges against income in each period. Special-purpose ratios, such as the times interest earned or the fixed charge coverage ratios, show the burden of fixed charges (such as interest or lease payments) and reveal whether the company is generating the earnings to pay them.

The proportion of income that interest and other fixed charges can safely consume varies from industry to industry. The ratios are used as general guidelines, similar to those used by a bank to say a consumer's house payment or car payment should be no more than a certain proportion of the consumer's income.

As the proportion of debt rises, creditors become more reluctant to lend and, eventually, credit will be available only at very high interest rates. Still, a certain amount of debt is good for owners because managers use debt to increase ROE.

ROI, Solvency, and ROE

We know that investment turnover times profit margin equals ROI. By adding a solvency ratio, we can add information and expand these basic components to analyze ROE as well as ROI. The solvency ratio that we add is total investment in assets divided by owners' equity. When we add the solvency ratio to ROI, algebraically we get ROE.

$$\text{Investment turnover} \times \text{Profit margin on sales} = \text{ROI}$$

$$\text{Investment turnover} \times \text{Profit margin on sales} \times \text{Solvency} = \text{ROE}$$

$$\frac{\text{Sales}}{\text{Investment}} \times \frac{\text{Income}}{\text{Sales}} \times \frac{\text{Investment}}{\text{Owners' equity}} = \text{ROE}$$

In Chapter 2, we reproduced the balance sheets and income statements of MCI Communications and RJR Nabisco, and we determined that the investment turnovers, profit margins, and ROIs for these companies are as follows.

	Investment turnover	×	Profit margin	= ROI
MCI	0.109 times	×	0.815	= 0.089
RJR Nabisco	0.489 times	×	0.166	= 0.081

Comparing Solvency Ratios

The solvency ratios for MCI and RJR Nabisco are shown below. The amounts are taken from Exhibits 2–1 and 2–2.

$$\frac{\text{Investment}}{\text{Owners' equity}} = \text{Solvency ratio}$$

$$\text{MCI } \frac{\$16,366}{\$9,004} = 1.818$$

$$\text{RJR Nabisco } \frac{\$31,408}{\$10,908} = 2.879$$

What do these solvency ratios mean? One conclusion we draw is that RJR Nabisco is much more heavily leveraged than MCI. RJR Nabisco uses debt to build investment to almost three times owners'

27

equity, while MCI uses debt to build investment to less than two times owners' equity. The percent of investment financed by owners' equity is the inverse of the solvency ratio: 1 divided by 1.818 = 55 percent for MCI, and 1 divided by 2.879 = 34.7 percent for RJR Nabisco. Thus, debt financed 45 percent (1 − .55) of the investment for MCI and 65.3 percent (1 − .347) for RJR Nabisco.

Leveraging ROE

How does this difference in leverage affect ROE? When we add leverage to our ROI components, we find MCI's 8.9 percent ROI resulting in only a 16.2 percent ROE, while RJR Nabisco's slightly lower 8.1 percent ROI is leveraged by the use of debt to an ROE of 23.3 percent.

	Investment turnover	×	Profit margin	×	Solvency	= ROE
MCI	0.109 times	×	0.815	×	1.818	= 0.162
RJR Nabisco	0.489 times	×	0.166	×	2.879	= 0.233

How good is an ROE of 16 percent or 20 percent? When the average ROE of the Standard & Poor's 500 companies reached 20.12 percent in the first quarter of 1995—the highest level since World War II—the *Wall Street Journal* said an ROE of 20 percent was equivalent to a baseball player hitting .350.[1] However, the *Wall Street Journal* was speaking of ROE calculated using *net income after tax* rather than *operating earnings,* which we used in our calculations. When we determine ROE using net income, activities and events other than operations cause ROE for MCI to be 8.8 percent, and ROE for RJR Nabisco to be 4.75 percent.

So, who has a 20 percent ROE?

The income statement and balance sheet for Wal-Mart Stores are shown in Exhibit 3–1. Using bottom-line net income, Wal-Mart's

---

[1] Roger Lowenstein, "The '20% Club' No Longer Is Exclusive" (Intrinsic Value), *Wall Street Journal,* May 4, 1995, C1.

profit margin on sales is 3.5 percent, its investment turnover is 2.54, and its ratio of investment to owners' equity is 2.46. Wal-Mart's 1994 ROI was 8.8 percent and its ROE was 21.7 percent.

Some companies do even better. The 1994 income statement and balance sheet for Coca-Cola Company are in Exhibit 3–2. Again using net income rather than operating earnings, Coca-Cola has a profit margin on sales of 15.5 percent, an investment turnover of 1.17, and a ratio of investment to owners' equity of 2.65. Coca-Cola's ROI is 18.4 percent and its ROE is an astounding 48.8 percent. (The

EXHIBIT 3–1
Consolidated Statements of Income for Wal-Mart Stores

(Amounts in thousands, except per share data.) Fiscal year ended January 31,	1994	1993	1992
Revenues:			
Net Sales	$67,344,574	$55,483,771	$43,886,902
Rentals from licensed departments	47,422	36,035	28,659
Other income—net	593,548	464,758	373,862
	67,985,544	55,984,564	44,289,423
Cost and Expenses:			
Cost of sales	53,443,743	44,174,685	34,786,119
Operating, selling, and general and administrative expenses	10,333,218	8,320,842	6,684,304
Interests Costs:			
Debt	331,308	142,649	113,305
Capital leases	185,697	180,049	152,558
	64,293,966	52,818,225	41,736,286
Income Before Income Taxes	3,691,578	3,166,339	2,553,137
Provision for Income Taxes:			
Current	1,324,777	1,136,918	906,183
Deferred	33,524	34,627	38,478
	1,358,301	1,171,545	944,661
Net Income	$ 2,333,277	$ 1,994,794	$ 1,608,476
Net Income Per Share	$ 1.02	$ .87	$ .70

(continued)

EXHIBIT 3–1 (continued)
Consolidated Balance Sheets for Wal-Mart Stores

(Amounts in thousands.)

January 31,	1994	1993
Assets		
Current Assets:		
Cash and cash equivalents	$ 20,115	$ 12,363
Receivables	689,987	524,555
Recoverable costs from sale/leaseback	208,236	312,016
Inventories:		
At replacement cost	11,483,119	9,779,981
Less LIFO reserve	469,413	511,672
LIFO	11,013,706	9,268,309
Prepaid expenses and other	182,558	80,347
Total Current Assets	12,114,602	10,197,590
Property, Plant and Equipment, at Cost:		
Land	2,740,883	1,692,510
Buildings and improvements	6,818,479	4,641,009
Fixtures and equipment	3,980,674	3,417,230
Transportation equipment	259,537	111,151
	13,799,573	9,861,900
Less accumulated depreciation	2,172,808	1,607,623
Net property, plant, and equipment	11,626,765	8,254,277
Property under capital leases	2,058,588	1,986,104
Less accumulated amortization	509,987	447,500
Net property under capital leases	1,548,601	1,538,604
Other Assets and Deferred Charges	1,150,796	574,616
Total Assets	$26,440,764	$20,565,087
Liabilities and Shareholders' Equity		
Current Liabilities:		
Commercial paper	$ 1,575,029	$ 1,588,825
Accounts payable	4,103,878	3,873,331
Accrued liabilities	1,473,198	1,042,108
Accrued federal and state income taxes	183,031	190,620
Long-term debt due within one year	19,658	13,849
Obligations under capital leases due within one year	51,429	45,553
Total Current Liabilities	7,406,223	6,754,286
Long-Term Debt	6,155,894	3,072,835
Long-Term Obligations Under Capital Leases	1,804,300	1,772,152
Deferred Income Taxes	321,909	206,634
Shareholders' Equity:		
Preferred stock ($.10 par value; 100,000 shares authorized, none issued)		
Common stock ($.10 par value; 5,500,000 shares authorized, 2,298,769 and 2,299,638 issued and outstanding in 1994 and 1993, respectively)	229,877	229,964
Capital in excess of par value	535,639	526,647
Retained earnings	9,986,922	8,002,569
Total Shareholders' Equity	10,752,438	8,759,180
Total Liabilities and Shareholders' Equity	$26,440,764	$20,565,087

30

EXHIBIT 3–2
Consolidated Statements of Income for the
Coca-Cola Company and Subsidiaries

Year Ended December 31,	1994	1993	1992
(In millions except per share data)			
Net Operating Revenues	$16,172	$13,957	$13,074
Cost of goods sold	6,167	5,160	5,055
Gross Profit	10,005	8,797	8,019
Selling, administrative and general expenses	6,297	5,695	5,249
Operating Income	3,708	3,102	2,770
Interest income	181	144	164
Interest expense	199	168	171
Equity income	134	91	65
Other income (deductions)—net	(96)	4	(82)
Gain on issuance of stock by Coca-Cola Amatil	—	12	$ —
Income before Income Taxes and Changes in Accounting Principles	3,728	3,185	2,746
Income taxes	1,174	997	863
Income before Changes in Accounting Principles	2,554	2,188	1,883
Transition effects of changes in accounting principles			
Postemployment benefits	—	(12)	—
Postretirement benefits other than pensions			
Consolidated operations	—	—	(146)
Equity investments	—	—	(73)
Net Income	$ 2,554	$ 2,176	$ 1,664
Income per Share			
Before changes in accounting principles	$ 1.98	$ 1.68	$ 1.43
Transition effects of changes in accounting principles			
Postemployment benefits	—	(.01)	—
Postretirement benefits other than pensions			
Consolidated operations	—	—	(.11)
Equity investments	—	—	(.06)
Net Income per Share	$ 1.98	$ 1.67	$ 1.26
Average Shares Outstanding	1,290	1,302	1,317

(continued)

EXHIBIT 3–2 (continued)
Consolidated Balance Sheets for the
Coca-Cola Company and Subsidiaries

December 31,	1994	1993
(In millions except share data)		
Assets		
Current		
Cash and cash equivalents	$ 1,386	$ 998
Marketable securities	145	80
	1,531	1,078
Trade accounts receivable, less allowances of $33 in 1994 and $39 in 1993	1,470	1,210
Finance subsidiary receivables	55	33
Inventories	1,047	1,049
Prepaid expenses and other assets	1,102	1,064
Total Current Assets	5,205	4,434
Investments and Other Assets		
Equity method investments		
Coca-Cola Enterprises Inc.	524	498
Coca-Cola Amatil Limited	694	592
Other, principally bottling companies	1,114	1,037
Cost method investments, principally bottling companies	178	88
Finance subsidiary receivables	255	226
Marketable securities and other assets	1,163	868
	3,928	3,309
Property, Plant and Equipment		
Land	221	197
Buildings and improvements	1,814	1,616
Machinery and equipment	3,776	3,380
Containers	346	403
	6,157	5,596
Less allowances for depreciation	2,077	1,867
	4,080	3,729
Goodwill and Other Intangible Assets	660	549
	$13,873	$12,021

Coca-Cola Company is examined in more detail in Chapter 21.) Here are the calculations on the two companies:

	Investment turnover	×	Profit margin	×	Solvency	= ROE
Wal-Mart	2.54	×	0.035	×	2.46	= 0.217
Coca-Cola	1.17	×	0.155	×	2.65	= 0.488

Notice the different approaches managers use to achieve profitability in these companies, operating in two completely different business environments. Both firms have solvency ratios of about 2.5; but Coca-Cola has a very high return on sales, and Wal-Mart has a very low return on sales. Wal-Mart, however, turns over total assets two and one-half times, while Coca-Cola turns assets only a little over one time. Each company's strategy is appropriate to its business environment and successful in its own way.

4

PROBLEMS WITH ROI IN SEGMENTS

*M*anagers and analysts like ROI because it is a percent and, thus, easy to understand and consistent with how a company measures its cost of capital. Because it is a ratio, ROI "normalizes" activities and makes dissimilar activities comparable. Large departments can be compared to small departments. Managers of different functions can be compared in a meaningful way. Top management uses ROI to compare segments of the company to each other, to outside companies, or to other investment opportunities. If the manager of the vacuum cleaner division creates a profit of $30,000,000 on an investment of $200,000,000, top management can compare those figures to the performance of the manager of the $500,000 broom division, which showed a profit of $100,000, or to the treasurer's investment of $100,000 in a certificate of deposit at the bank.

Activity	Investment	Profit
Vacuum cleaner manufacture	$200,000,000	$30,000,000
Broom manufacture	500,000	100,000
Temporary investment of excess cash	100,000	7,000

These three activities, of different size and type, are difficult to compare without calculating an ROI. Because of ROI's flexibility, top management, financial analysts, and potential investors frequently use it to evaluate and compare the economic performance of companies and their segments. With the ROI of each of the activities, it is easy to rank managers' performance.

Activity	ROI
Broom manufacture	20%
Vacuum cleaner manufacture	15%
Temporary investment of excess cash	7%

A Comprehensive Tool with Problems

ROI is a comprehensive measure that is affected by all of the business activities that normally determine financial health. ROI is increased or decreased by the level of operating expenses incurred, and by changes in either sales volume or price. The investment base can include capital investment in plant, property, and equipment, or current investments such as receivables and inventories. Many managers feel ROI is useful because it provides a means of monitoring the results of capital investment decisions: if a project doesn't earn its projected return, the manager's ROI goes down.

The advantages of ROI, introduced in Chapter 1, are summarized as follows:

- ROI is easy to understand.
- ROI is directly comparable to the cost of capital.
- ROI normalizes dissimilar activities so they can be compared.
- ROI is comprehensive, reflecting all aspects of a business.
- ROI shows the results of capital investment decisions.

Gearing Investment and Profit

ROI is often criticized as making a complex management process appear unrealistically simple. An ROI of 20 percent, for example, appears to mean that each $1.00 in assets provides profit of $0.20. A reduction of $1.00 in assets is accompanied by a $0.20 reduction in profit; a $1.00 increase in assets results in a $0.20 increase in profit. The relationship described by an ROI percentage implies that an increase or decrease in investment is "geared" to an increase or decrease in profits by the ROI ratio.

Although the gearing of profit and investment is to some extent true, the relationship between investment and profit is not constant over all the assets in a segment. If, for example, Division A has an ROI of 20 percent, it seems to follow that if Division A increases its investment in inventory or equipment by $100,000, the division return will increase by $20,000 ($100,000 × 20 percent). Likewise, if Division B has an ROI of 25 percent, an additional $100,000 investment in inventory or equipment for the division will return $25,000. Regardless of the type of investment—inventory, equipment, or whatever—the ROI relationship appears to predict what profit managers can expect.

However, this is not true.

Different types of investment have different effects on profit. For example, investments required by OSHA (for safety precautions) or by the EPA (for pollution control) may have no effect whatever on profits. Other investments may individually create an array of different returns, regardless of the entity's overall ROI. An investment in high-tech robotics for production, for example, may create a much higher ROI than an investment in higher inventory stocks.

Investment in Different Segments

Gearing investment and profit also implies that ROI is different in different segments for investment in identical assets (e.g., equipment or inventory). The ROI for the asset appears to be determined not by its nature and use, but by the ROI of the segment in which the investment is made. As we have seen in our example, inventory (or any other investment) is expected to return 20 percent in Division A, but 25 percent in Division B. As a result, justifying an increase in inventory to support sales requires a larger contribution to profit in one segment than in the other.

The change in profit that actually accompanies a change in inventory investment depends in part on the segment's inventory level before the change, not the ROI on the segment's existing mix of assets. For example, if insufficient inventory levels are increased, profit may increase because stockouts are prevented and customer choice is improved. However, increasing an inventory that is already at an optimum level may decrease profit as a result of increased carrying charges and obsolescence.

A series of costs fluctuate as an inventory level varies from low to high: the cost of stockouts and poor customer selection (higher at low inventory levels); the cost of insurance, taxes, and other carrying costs; and ordering and receiving costs. (Lower inventory levels require more frequent, smaller orders to maintain.) The total of these costs is usually greater at very low and very high inventory levels than at an intermediate, optimum level that balances the cost of stockouts against excess carrying costs. Exhibit 4–1 shows how a segment's total inventory costs might vary with inventory level. The effect of a change in inventory investment depends on the segment's position on this graph when the investment is made.

EXHIBIT 4–1
A Graph of Total Inventory Costs and Inventory Level

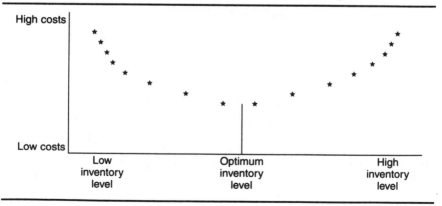

40

Requiring identical investments to pay their way with different returns in different segments of the company distorts the way managers make decisions. In a segment with a high ROI, for instance, there is an incentive for managers to lease assets that create low returns, even though other segments (with lower segment returns) routinely purchase the same assets. Again, assume Division A has an ROI of 20 percent, Division B an ROI of 25 percent. The cost of capital to the company is 18 percent, and both divisions need new warehouses. Each warehouse is expected to generate an ROI of 22 percent on the $100,000 invested. (The cost of capital is discussed in Chapter 15.) Division A will buy a warehouse because the 22 percent return will-increase the segment return, but Division B will lease a warehouse because the same return lowers its ROI. Here is how the decisions are reached.

	Division A	*Division B*
Assets	$1,000,000	$1,000,000
Profit	200,000	250,000
ROI	20%	25%
Plus new warehouse	100,000	100,000
New assets	1,100,000	1,100,000
Plus added profit	22,000	22,000
New profit	222,000	272,000
New ROI	20.18%	24.72%
Change in ROI	Increased 0.18%	Decreased 0.28%
Decision	Buy warehouse	Lease warehouse

In both cases, the return generated by the warehouse is greater than the company's cost of capital, and purchasing the warehouse would benefit the company. (From the company's perspective, a $100,000 warehouse investment yields a 22 percent return with only an 18 percent cost of capital in either case.) Division A's actions are congruent with the company's goal of increasing profit; Division B's are not.

41

ROI Targets Create Problems

In an attempt to be fair, top managers in some companies establish a single ROI target for all segment managers. However, when all segments have the same target ROI, the process is unfair, because of the factors just discussed. Consider, for example, a company that has four operating segments. Three of the segments are appliance stores, and the fourth is the company's customer credit granting segment.

Store A was built in 1970 with an investment of $100,000. Stores B and C were built two years ago. All three stores are identical, but, due to inflation, Stores B and C each cost $300,000 to build. All the stores carry an average appliance inventory costing $100,000. The investment in the credit granting segment consists of $50,000 in office equipment and computers in rented offices. Each of the stores earned a profit of $40,000 for the year and the credit office earned $3,000.

Store	A	B	C	Credit Office
Building and equipment	$100,000	$300,000	$300,000	$50,000
Inventory	100,000	100,000	100,000	NA
Total investment	$200,000	$400,000	$400,000	$50,000
Profit	$ 40,000	$ 40,000	$ 40,000	$ 3,000
ROI	20%	10%	10%	6%

Each store has an identical building and the same amount of inventory, and each generates the same profit. But, because the assets were acquired at different times, the old and new segment ROIs are not comparable in a meaningful way. The credit office creates an ROI of only 6 percent, but, because of its different asset mix and the different function it serves, it cannot be compared directly to the stores. The profit of the credit office depends on the other three segments' generation of credit sales. Likewise, the profit and ROI created by the stores depend on the ability to offer credit.

Because of the different ages of the stores and because the ROIs of the appliance stores and the credit office are not comparable, a single ROI target for all segments is neither practical nor useful.

Accounting Methods, Timing, and Manipulation

On another level, managers may find that otherwise similar segments lack comparability because managers may use different accounting procedures, particularly for inventories and long-lived assets, which by themselves make accounting earnings different. Choosing LIFO rather than FIFO inventory accounting, or accelerated rather than straight-line depreciation will change accounting income substantially.

Other costs are subject to manipulation. A manager may delay or eliminate some crucial but routine maintenance procedures to lower costs and improve earnings in a slow period. Likewise, discretionary costs such as advertising or research might be delayed or eliminated. Production can be increased to lower the average overhead per unit, positions that are vacated can be left unfilled, and other counter-productive measures can be taken to increase profit and ROI in the short term.

At the extreme, segment managers may falsify records, increasing inventories to reduce cost of goods sold, or recording sales in the current year even though they were made after the year-end cut-off. Accounts found to be uncollectible may be retained on the books as good receivables and spoiled or obsolete inventory included as good.

Top management encourages manipulation and fraud by setting unrealistic ROI targets for segment managers.

5

HOW ROI AFFECTS
INVESTMENT AND
DISINVESTMENT
DECISIONS

The problem most commonly cited as accompanying the use of ROI is the refusal of managers to pursue investments that, though otherwise acceptable, reduce the manager's ROI. For example, a segment manager with a segment ROI of 25 percent may refuse to invest in a project or asset expected to return 20 percent, even if the company's cost of capital is only 15 percent, because the investment will lower the segment's ROI. (Cost of capital is discussed in Chapter 15.)

	Before New Project	*New Project*	*With New Project*
Investment	$500,000	$125,000	$625,000
Profit	125,000	25,000	150,000
ROI	25%	20%	24%

The same logic may lead a segment manager to increase ROI by disinvesting in assets that return less than the segment's ROI. Scrapping or selling otherwise profitable assets that return only 20 percent, when the segment's ROI is 24 percent, increases a manager's ROI.

	With Low ROI Project	*Project Scrapped*	*Without Project*
Investment	$625,000	$125,000	$500,000
Profit	150,000	25,000	125,000
ROI	24%	20%	25%

In both cases, the project return is greater than the company's cost of capital and adds to the company's total dollars of profit. Segment managers may be discouraged from scrapping or selling lower-return assets because disinvestment is generally obvious to top management, but forgoing investment opportunities is not. Top managers often learn of only the opportunities disclosed to them by segment managers. If a segment manager does not present a project, top management may never learn of it.

A manager's decision to reject a 20 percent ROI project and to disinvest in a 20 percent asset because of a higher segment ROI is suboptimal behavior for the company as a whole. However, segment managers who reject projects or disinvest assets are acting rationally from their own perspective, by maintaining or increasing the ROI of their segments. If top management is to avoid segment-oriented ROIs, there must be goals for segment managers other than a target or maximum ROI.

Profit-Neutral, Nondiscretionary Investments

Many nondiscretionary investments do not create increases in profit. Examples of such profit-neutral investments include replacing or upgrading administrative or support facilities (i.e., buildings or parking lots) and adding equipment because of OSHA regulations or EPA requirements.

Some managers argue that because these nondiscretionary projects require capital but do not return capital, other projects must return significantly more than a company's cost of capital. Thus, pushing managers toward projects that earn substantially more than the cost of capital is beneficial because the returns of profitable operations must be sufficient to cover the cost of capital invested in nondiscretionary projects that create no returns.

If a company with a $1,000,000 investment in assets has a 15 percent cost of capital, any return above 15 percent results in profit. An ROI of 17 percent gives a profit of $170,000.

Assets	$1,000,000
Profit at 17% ROI in assets	170,000
Cost of capital at 15% of $1,000,000	150,000
Profit in excess of the cost of capital	20,000

However, if $200,000 of the company's investment in assets is in nondiscretionary, profit-neutral projects, leaving productive assets of only $800,000, a return of 17 percent on productive assets is not enough to cover the cost of capital.

Total assets	$1,000,000
Nondiscretionary, profit-neutral assets	200,000
Productive assets	$ 800,000
Profit at 17% ROI in productive assets	136,000
Cost of capital at 15% of $1,000,000	150,000
Excess of the cost of capital over profit	14,000

In order for this company to avoid a loss, the ROI for productive assets must be 18.75 percent or greater. A hurdle rate is the rate a project must clear to produce a return when all investments are considered. The hurdle rate can be equal to, or greater than, the cost of capital. (The cost of capital is discussed in Chapter 15, and more sophisticated capital project selection techniques are discussed in Chapters 17 and 18.)

Productive assets	$ 800,000
Nondiscretionary, profit-neutral assets	200,000
Total assets	$1,000,000
Profit at 18.75% ROI in productive assets	150,000
Cost of capital at 15% of $1,000,000	150,000
Profit and cost of capital are equal	0

As noted in Chapter 19, managers often make poor investment decisions using an ROI (accounting return) model rather than a discounted cash flow model. Realizing that some assets create no profit is only part of the problem.

Residual Income

One approach to avoiding the incongruent goals of segment managers who seek to avoid projects that have a lower ROI than the segment ROI is to use residual income (RI) in addition to (or in place of) ROI. All capital has a cost. There is a weighted cost of capital for the company's funds, and segment managers are often charged for capital committed to their segments. RI looks at the profit contributed by a project above its cost of capital. If the project used in our beginning-of-the-chapter illustration is examined on the basis of a 15 percent cost of capital, the segment manager realizes that adopting the project increases total earnings. The $6,250 increase in RI justifies the reduction in ROI.

	Before New Project	*New Project*	*With New Project*
Investment	$500,000	$125,000	$625,000
Profit	125,000	25,000	150,000
Cost of capital at 15%	75,000	18,750	93,750
Residual income (above cost of capital)	$ 50,000	$ 6,250	$ 56,250
ROI	25%	20%	24%

If management has realized that all investments must return more than a hurdle rate of 18.75 percent, that rate is used to calculate RI instead of the company's cost of capital. Again, the RI produced by the project justifies the investment.

	Before New Project	New Project	With New Project
Investment	$500,000	$125,000	$625,000
Profit	125,000	25,000	150,000
Hurdle rate at 18.75%	93,750	23,437	117,187
Residual income (above hurdle rate)	$ 56,250	$ 1,563	$ 32,813
ROI	25%	20%	24%

One problem with using RI for performance measurement is that it is difficult to make comparisons among segments of different sizes. Large segments should generate larger amounts of RI than small segments. In these cases, using a budgeted or target RI for each segment compensates for size differences—but a budgeted ROI that recognizes the value of the 20 percent project accomplishes the same thing.

Multiple Returns

Another approach to establishing a target ROI for a segment or a proposed project is to use a different required or hurdle ROI for each type of asset. When this is done, the rates reflect the idea that investment in some assets is riskier than investment in others, and thus should create higher returns. To illustrate this approach, assume the project in our previous example (a $125,000 investment with a $25,000 expected return) had the following proposed asset mix.

Facilities	$ 50,000
Computers	40,000
Inventory	15,000
Receivables	10,000
Cash	10,000
Total	$125,000

Top managers, considering the relative risk and the company's cost of capital, have decided that an investment in facilities is acceptable if it returns 15 percent or more. But, using the same logic, they also feel an investment in computers should return at least 30 percent because of the high risk of technical obsolescence. Investment in inventory is expected to return 20 percent, but because of the risk of uncollectibles, receivables should return 25 percent. Holding cash, like owning facilities, carries low risk and requires a minimum return of only 15 percent. The profit this project must create is determined as follows.

Facilities	$ 50,000 × 0.15 =	$ 7,500
Computers	40,000 × 0.30 =	12,000
Inventory	15,000 × 0.20 =	3,000
Receivables	10,000 × 0.25 =	2,500
Cash	10,000 × 0.15 =	1,500
Total	$125,000	$26,500

The required ROI for this project is 21.2 percent ($26,500 ÷ $125,000). This rate is greater than the expected ROI of 20 percent ($25,000 ÷ $125,000), and the project is rejected. The project's residual income is negative, also leading to rejection.

Required return	$26,500
Expected return	25,000
Residual income	($ 1,500)

Suppose the proposed project could be restructured, perhaps by using some computer capacity already owned. This would reduce the investment in computers by half, lower the project's risk, turn its RI to positive, and make its ROI acceptable. With the investment reduced, the required ROI is 19.5 percent and the expected ROI (based on the new investment) is 23.8 percent.

Facilities	$ 50,000 × 0.15 =	$ 7,500
Computers	20,000 × 0.30 =	6,000
	($ 40,000 × 50%)	
Inventory	15,000 × 0.20 =	3,000
Receivables	10,000 × 0.25 =	2,500
Cash	10,000 × 0.15 =	1,500
Total	$105,000	$20,500

$$\text{Required ROI} = \frac{\$20,500}{\$105,000} = 0.195$$

$$\text{Expected ROI} = \frac{\$25,000}{\$105,000} = 0.238$$

Required return	$20,500
Expected return	25,000
Residual income	$ 4,500

As a device for assessing proposed additions to assets, RI may still discourage some managers because many projects will have low or negative residual income during the first few years. However, first-year losses are a limitation of ROI as well. Both measures focus on short-term performance and do not consider how well a project accomplishes long-term goals.

Funds for a Particular Project

There is a tendency for some managers to use the cost of capital associated with each individual asset as that asset's minimum required rate of return. This is a mistake. The required minimum return should be determined by considering the weighted average cost of all capital and the risk of the individual investments. Consider inventory, for example: from a financing standpoint, the funds for purchased inventory (such as raw material) are sometimes obtained cost-free by using vendors' credit terms, yet it is foolish to assert that the company needs no return for the risk assumed by investing in inventories.

Additionally, equally risky investments (perhaps in identical facilities for two different segments) do not justify different required rates of return simply because they are financed at different costs. The nature of the investment, not the source of financing, determines the risk and, thus, the minimum return. Facilities financed by owner investment are not riskier than facilities financed by debt, even though owners generally demand higher returns than do creditors.

Residual Income Return on Investment

Some companies use a performance index based on RI as a percentage of investment. This ratio is derived from a desire to have the benefits of RI and ROI in a single measure, but it fails. Like ROI, the hybrid measure appears to normalize unlikes and to have intuitive meaning, but the relationship is artificial and gives rise only to contrived interpretations.

For the illustration of the restructured project, the ratio (which has no name) is as follows.

$$\text{Ratio} = \frac{\text{Residual income}}{\text{Investment}}$$

$$\text{Ratio} = \frac{\$4{,}500}{\$105{,}000}$$

$$\text{Ratio} = 0.0429$$

What does this mean? Only that residual income is 4.29 percent of the investment base. Any additional interpretation is meaningless.

ROI and Budgeting

When a company's managers are aware of the problems ROI may cause, these problems tend to disappear. The planning process in most companies provides a strong argument that the incentive provided by

ROI for segment managers to ignore company goals and avoid some profitable investments is actually no problem at all when ROI is understood. In their annual planning, managers first budget sales prices and quantities, then the costs of the planned sales and the other operating costs that must be incurred. Profit is determined from the budgets of sales and expenses. Next, managers determine the investment in inventory and other assets necessary to support the planned sales activity. Asset additions are usually budgeted using net present values (NPV) of cash flows (as in Chapters 16 and 17) rather than ROI targets.

When the planning process is complete, budgeted profit divided by the budgeted asset base determines the segment's target ROI. However, budgeted ROI is a target only to the extent that all the budgeted items that compose it are targets. Budgeted ROI targets may be lower than the actual ROI of current and past years, thus allowing managers to accept projects with a return between the cost of capital and the segment's ROI.

When budgets are used to evaluate managers' performance, the assessment is most often based on the manager's ability to establish a workable budget (usually in negotiation with the manager's superior) and then accomplish the goals the budget describes. When this is done, segment managers can be evaluated by comparing actual ROI to budgeted ROI instead of by ranking segment ROIs. Budgeting that incorporates a target ROI allows top management to consider the profit potential of each segment, and allows segment managers to invest in assets that increase RI, even if they reduce ROI.

6

DETERMINING PROFIT AND THE INVESTMENT BASE

*W*hen companies use ROI to evaluate segments, managers must decide on the composition of the return and investment they will use. Several forms of profit and investment can be identified, depending on the goal of the evaluation. For instance, is top management evaluating the economic performance of the segment, or the managerial performance of the segment manager? They are not the same thing. Economic performance evaluation of the segment calls for classifying certain components of profit and the asset base differently from the classification required for management performance evaluation.

If segment economic performance is assessed, the segment should bear all costs directly associated with its operation and all investment dedicated to its mission, regardless of who controls the costs or manages the investment base. The inclusion of allocated costs is discretionary. In contrast, if the goal is to assess the manager's performance, only the components of profit and the investment base controlled by the manager should be included. All other cost should be excluded.

What Profit Measure?

In published financial statements, profit is determined using generally accepted accounting principles (GAAP), and the performance of segments is calculated in the same way. Exhibit 6–1 shows the ROI (here called return on average assets) of the forty subsidiaries (segments) of Mercantile Bancorporation Incorporated as listed in

EXHIBIT 6–1
ROI of Subsidiaries of Mercantile Bancorporation
Incorporated, from 1994 Annual Report

Bank	Chief Executive Officer
Mercantile Bank of St. Louis N.A.	Thomas H. Jacobsen
Mercantile Bank of Kansas City	Richard C. King
Mercantile Bank of Kansas	Richard C. King
Mercantile Bank of Illinois N.A.	A. Jesse Hopkins
Mercantile Bank of Joplin	Larry L. Gilb
Mercantile Bank of Northern Iowa	Daniel B. Watters
Mercantile Bank of St. Joseph	Thomas B. Fitzsimmons
Mercantile Bank of Springfield	David W. Felske
Mercantile Bank of Lawrence	John R. Elmore
Mercantile Bank of Jefferson County	William C. Heady
Mercantile Bank of Topeka	Charles N. Johns
Mercantile Bank of Cape Girardeau	O. J. Miller
Mercantile Bank of Franklin County	Thomas M. Metzger
Mercantile Bank of the Mineral Area	Lowell C. Peterson
Mercantile Bank of North Central Missouri	Loren E. Jensen
Mercantile Bank of West Central Missouri	Phillip M. Hunt
Mercantile Bank of Lake of the Ozarks	Jerry A. Setser
Mercantile Bank of Poplar Bluff	Melvin D. Brown
Mercantile Bank of Mt. Vernon	David P. Strautz
Mercantile Bank of Centralia	Harry N. Harrison
Mercantile Bank of Missouri Valley	R. Scott Weston
Mercantile Bank of Stoddard/Bollinger Counties	John S. Davis
Mercantile Bank of Monett	Jerry L. LeClair
Mercantile Bank of Trenton	Jan O. Humphreys
Mercantile Bank of Perryville	Mark D. Grieshaber
Mercantile Bank of Flora	Martin P. Tudor
Mercantile Bank of Phelps County	Robert R. Thompson
Mercantile Bank of Pike County	Darrell L. Denish
Mercantile Bank of Memphis	Robert L. Henselman
Mercantile Bank of Doniphan	William R. Orendorff
Mercantile Bank of Boone County	Terry W. Coffelt
Mercantile Bank of East Central Missouri	Stanley B. Bonnes
Mercantile Bank of Ste. Genevieve	Samuel F. Berendzen
Mercantile Bank of Northwest Missouri	Coby D. Lamb
Mercantile Bank of Willow Springs	Jerry H. Abbott
Mercantile Bank of Sikeston	Mark E. Nelson
Mercantile Bank of Wright County	Thomas F. Zinnert
Mercantile Bank of Carlyle	Gregory A. Meyer
Mercantile Bank of Plattsburg	Alan L. Hall
Mercantile Trust Company N.A.	W. Randolph Adams

| Locations | | December 31, 1994 ($ in Thousands) | | |
Main Office	Total	Assets	Shareholder's Equity	Return on Average Assets
St. Louis, MO	54	$6,351,671	$524,064	1.31%
Kansas City, MO	17	777,385	69,778	1.31
Overland Park, KS	18	590,521	49,350	1.21
Alton, IL	15	455,261	35,565	2.42
Joplin, MO	11	387,641	34,526	1.70
Waterloo, IA	7	364,669	31,813	1.28
St. Joseph, MO	9	329,228	28,770	1.33
Springfield, MO	9	305,782	24,773	1.66
Lawrence, KS	12	233,657	24,310	1.51
High Ridge, MO	5	211,200	18,723	1.60
Topeka, KS	12	197,692	17,244	1.16
Cape Girardeau, MO	3	170,976	13,208	1.18
Washington, MO	4	161,611	13,020	1.74
Farmington, MO	3	160,033	13,138	2.05
Macon, MO	5	157,904	13,229	1.50
Sedalia, MO	8	147,535	14,464	1.18
Eldon, MO	4	124,501	11,118	1.68
Poplar Bluff, MO	4	104,210	9,230	1.37
Mt. Vernon, IL	5	91,630	8,107	1.11
Centralia, IL	3	91,419	9,811	1.35
Richmond, MO	2	86,618	7,313	1.33
Dexter, MO	4	79,511	6,763	1.43
Monett, MO	5	79,228	6,971	1.48
Trenton, MO	3	78,572	9,824	1.36
Perryville, MO	1	69,163	6,198	1.35
Flora, IL	1	68,242	8,668	1.27
Rolla, MO	2	67,161	5,468	.99
Bowling Green, MO	2	58,020	4,512	1.38
Memphis, MO	1	51,304	4,331	2.10
Doniphan, MO	2	50,292	5,080	1.54
Columbia, MO	2	49,564	4,000	.73
Montgomery City, MO	2	49,051	4,154	1.66
Ste. Genevieve, MO	1	48,125	4,034	1.14
Maryville, MO	4	43,358	4,463	.95
Willow Springs, MO	1	39,195	3,504	2.31
Sikeston, MO	1	39,161	3,665	1.34
Hartville, MO	1	38,443	3,385	1.49
Carlyle, IL	3	37,975	3,842	1.04
Plattsburg, MO	3	37,288	3,836	1.56
St. Louis, MO	—	8,002	7,471	—

its 1994 annual report. Mercantile gives no segment information other than total assets, shareholders' equity, and ROI (determined using GAAP).

Most companies provide the type of segment disclosure shown in Exhibit 6–2, which presents segment information from RJR Nabisco's 1994 annual report. RJR Nabisco shows net sales, operating income, capital expenditures, depreciation expense, and assets for its tobacco and food operations. It also shows net sales, operating income, and assets, separated into geographic segments. The ROI for each business segment can be calculated from the information provided in the annual report.

Evaluating Managers Rather Than Segments

Both Mercantile Bancorporation and RJR Nabisco present the GAAP-based information useful for stockholders and others in assessing the performance of the company's operating segments. However, this information is *not* useful in assessing the performance of segment managers. Companies that use ROI to assess the performance of managers, rather than segments, often exclude one or more of the following in segment operating expenses: income taxes, interest on corporate debt, allocated costs (of administration or other activities), or any other costs the segment manager does not control.

Some companies argue that charging a share of interest expense to a segment makes managers aware that invested funds are not free. If there is no obvious cost, they claim, segment managers may tend to use more funds than they otherwise would. Still, because it ignores the cost of owners' equity, an interest charge understates the true cost of capital, which includes the cost of both debt and owners' equity. (This understatement is in all income statements.) Others insist that if managers realize (as they do) that invested funds must recover the unstated cost of equity capital, they also realize that the cost of creditor capital must be recovered, even in the absence of a stated interest charge.

EXHIBIT 6–2
RJR Nabisco Segment Disclosure from 1994 Annual Report

	Year Ended December 31, 1994	Year Ended December 31, 1993	Year Ended December 31, 1992
Net sales:			
Tobacco	$ 7,667	$ 8,079	$ 9,027
Food	7,699	7,025	6,707
Consolidated net sales	$15,366	$15,104	$15,734
Operating income:			
Tobacco (1)(2)	$ 1,826	$ 893	$ 2,241
Food (1)(2)	931	624	769
Headquarters (2)	(207)	(139)	(112)
Consolidated operating income	$ 2,550	$ 1,378	$ 2,898
Capital expenditures:			
Tobacco	$ 215	$ 224	$ 189
Food	455	391	330
Consolidated capital expenditures	$ 670	$ 615	$ 519
Depreciation expense:			
Tobacco	$ 228	$ 237	$ 252
Food	218	207	197
Headquarters	8	4	6
Consolidated depreciation expense	$ 454	$ 448	$ 455

	December 31, 1994	December 31, 1993
Assets:		
Tobacco	$19,420	$19,904
Food	11,917	11,270
Headquarters (3)	71	121
Consolidated assets	$31,408	$31,295

(1) Includes amortization of trademarks and goodwill for Tobacco and Food, respectively, for the year ended December 31, 1994, of $404 million and $225 million; for the year ended December 31, 1993, of $407 million and $218 million and for the year ended December 31, 1992, of $404 million and $212 million.

(2) The 1993 and 1992 amounts include the effects of the restructuring expense of Tobacco (1993—$544 million; 1992—$43 million), Food (1993—$153 million; 1992—$63 million) and Headquarters (1993—$33 million; 1992—$0), and the 1992 gain ($98 million) from the sale of Holdings' ready-to-eat cold cereal business (See Note 1 to the Consolidated Financial Statements).

(3) Cash and cash equivalents for the domestic operating companies are included in the Headquarters' assets.

What Investment?

There are three main questions to answer in determining the investment amount to use in an ROI calculation.

1. What assets should be included?
2. What liabilities should be deducted?
3. How should the assets be valued?

The remainder of this chapter discusses the first two questions. Valuing assets is discussed in the next chapter.

What Assets Should Be Included?

The question of what assets to include is answered, in part, by deciding whether top management is evaluating a segment's manager or the economic performance of the segment. The issue is much the same for investment as it is for profit. If the economic performance of the segment is being assessed, segment investment should include all capital dedicated to its mission, regardless of who manages the capital. If the segment manager's performance is being assessed, only those components of investment controlled by the manager should be included.

The question, however, is broader than defining the entity to be evaluated. Another common problem is determining the treatment of shared assets. This is a problem analogous to allocating shared expenses in determining operating income.

Shared assets can include a common pool of cash and receivables. Most companies do not include shared facilities in the investment base, but many include cash and receivables. For example, if headquarters sets the company's credit policy and is responsible for collecting receivables, and if company cash is centrally controlled, should cash and receivables be in a segment's assets base? Because it is difficult to determine appropriate amounts of cash or receivables for each segment, some companies include cash and receivables at arbitrary amounts, such as cash equal to two weeks' payables, or receivables equal to two months' sales.

What Liabilities Should Be Deducted?

Regardless of the assets included, at least three variations of investment are created by subtracting different liabilities. Each variation stems from a different conception of investment and results in a different ROI. All investment variations can be used for either the company as a whole or for segments within the company. Exhibit 6–3 contains the 1994 income statement and balance sheet of HON Industries. The amounts in Exhibit 6–3 are used to calculate the following three returns (in each case, we use net income as the numerator).

1. **Total assets.** This measure does not deduct liabilities and gives an ROI sometimes called return on assets (ROA).

Net income divided by	$ 54,156,000
Total assets	$372,568,000
ROI (ROA)	14.54%

2. **Total assets minus current liabilities.** Subtracting current liabilities from total assets gives a return on all funds committed for the long term. This measure of ROI is important to top management.

Net income divided by		$ 54,156,000
Total assets minus	$372,568,000	
Current liabilities	111,093,000	261,475,000
ROI		20.71%

3. **Total assets minus all liabilities.** This measure gives a return on net assets or on owners' equity, sometimes called ROE. ROE is often used by shareholders or their analysts. (For further discussion see Chapters 3 and 21.)

EXHIBIT 6–3
Consolidated Statements of Income for HON
Industries Inc. and Subsidiaries

For the Years	1994	1993	1992
Net sales	$845,998,000	$780,326,000	$706,550,000
Cost of products sold	573,392,000	537,828,000	479,179,000
Gross Profit	272,606,000	242,498,000	227,371,000
Selling and administrative expenses	185,490,000	171,048,000	165,075,000
Operating Income	87,116,000	71,450,000	62,296,000
Interest income	2,470,000	2,524,000	3,038,000
Interest expense	3,248,000	3,120,000	3,441,000
Income Before Income Taxes	86,338,000	70,854,000	61,893,000
Income taxes	31,945,000	26,216,000	23,210,000
Income Before Cumulative Effect of Accounting Changes	54,393,000	44,638,000	38,683,000
Cumulative effect of accounting changes	(237,000)	489,000	—
Net Income	$ 54,156,000	$ 45,127,000	$ 38,683,000
Net Income per Common Share:			
Income before cumulative effect of accounting changes	$ 1.74	$ 1.39	$ 1.18
Cumulative effect of accounting changes	(.01)	.02	—
Net Income	$ 1.73	$ 1.41	$ 1.18

(continued)

EXHIBIT 6–3 (continued)
Consolidated Balance Sheets for HON Industries Inc. and Subsidiaries

As of Year-End	1994	1993	1992
Assets			
Current Assets			
Cash and cash equivalents	$ 27,659,000	$ 32,778,000	$ 40,069,000
Short-term investments	3,083,000	11,598,000	5,872,000
Receivables	94,269,000	83,650,000	78,857,000
Inventories	43,259,000	38,630,000	30,262,000
Deferred income taxes	11,565,000	11,304,000	11,439,000
Prepaid expenses and other current assets	8,975,000	10,459,000	4,810,000
Total Current Assets	188,810,000	188,419,000	171,309,000
Property, Plant, and Equipment	177,844,000	157,770,000	145,849,000
Other Assets	5,914,000	6,216,000	5,588,000
Total Assets	$372,568,000	$352,405,000	$322,746,000
Liabilities and Shareholders' Equity			
Current Liabilities			
Accounts payable and accrued expenses	$ 99,898,000	$ 97,205,000	$ 78,904,000
Income taxes	4,949,000	6,936,000	5,750,000
Note payable and current maturities of long-term obligations	6,246,000	6,618,000	7,126,000
Total Current Liabilities	111,093,000	110,759,000	91,780,000
Long-Term Debt and Other Liabilities	46,080,000	45,260,000	46,519,000
Capital Lease Obligations	8,661,000	5,854,000	7,721,000
Deferred Income Taxes	12,094,000	10,979,000	13,717,000
Shareholders' Equity			
Common stock	30,675,000	31,676,000	32,369,000
Paid-in capital	434,000	281,000	2,580,000
Retained earnings	174,642,000	161,079,000	143,741,000
Receivable from HON Members Company Ownership Plan	(11,111,000)	(13,483,000)	(15,681,000)
Total Shareholders' Equity	194,640,000	179,553,000	163,009,000
Total Liabilities and Shareholders' Equity	$372,568,000	$352,405,000	$322,746,000

Net income divided by		$ 54,156,000
Total assets minus	$372,568,000	
Total liabilities	177,928,000	194,640,000
ROI (ROE)		27.82%

Which Return Is Best?

Some managers of large segments might be able to borrow long-term directly or manage their own short-term payables. A segment might even be a subsidiary, with a full range of long- and short-term debt. In these cases, it makes good sense to subtract from its assets any debt a segment management controls. The company can then measure the return on its capital invested long-term in the segment. (This measurement is done, for example, by a parent company that calculates the ROE in its subsidiary company.)

Usually, however, ROA is the ROI measure best suited to investment centers because managers often don't know or care where their funds originate.

7

HOW TO VALUE THE
INVESTMENT BASE

Chapter 6 addressed the questions of what assets should be included and what liabilities should be deducted when determining the asset base of a segment. This chapter discusses optional responses to the question of how we should value the segment's assets. There are at least four approaches to valuing the assets included in the investment base.

1. **Gross book value.** The historical or acquisition cost of assets, without deducting accumulated depreciation, amortization, or depletion.

2. **Net book value.** Gross book value minus accumulated depreciation, amortization, and depletion. This is the most common valuation approach.

3. **Replacement cost.** The estimated cost of replacing the assets. Replacement cost sounds logical but has definitional and other problems, discussed later in this chapter.

4. **Economic value.** The present value of future cash flows. This method is rarely used.

Gross Book Value

Using the gross book value (BV) of the assets in the investment base gives managers an incentive to make unwise equipment disposal and replacement decisions.

Disposal Decisions

Managers who are evaluated by an ROI using gross book values have an incentive to (1) scrap old equipment that is fully depreciated, infrequently used, but still needed, and (2) scrap any equipment that is not returning a target ROI, regardless of condition. Even if scrapping equipment is foolish from the company's viewpoint and produces a loss on disposal for the segment, the disinvestment still improves the segment's ROI because it reduces the investment base (the denominator). The disposal will improve ROI even in the year of disposal, if the loss on disposal is less than the disposed asset's profit shortfall.

For example, Segment X has a piece of equipment, A, that returns less than the other assets.

	Segment X		
	Equipment A	*All Other Assets*	*Total for Segment*
Gross Book Value	$100,000	$500,000	$600,000
Profit	15,000	125,000	140,000
ROI	15%	25%	23.33%

Equipment A has a profit shortfall of $10,000. (A profit of $10,000 more, or $25,000, gives a return of 25 percent, equal to the return of the other assets.) Thus, if the loss on disposal of Equipment A is less than $10,000, segment ROI in the year of disposal is increased. If Equipment A is sold for a $5,000 loss on January 1 (before Equipment A makes any profit contribution), segment ROI still increases from 23.33 percent to 24 percent in the year of disposal, despite the loss of $15,000 profit the equipment would have earned if not disposed of.

Segment X

	Equipment A	All Other Assets
Gross Book Value	-0-	$500,000
Profit before loss	-0-	125,000
Disposal loss		(5,000)
Profit after loss		120,000
ROI		24%

In subsequent years, with Equipment A and its contribution to profit gone, the Segment X operating profit is reduced by $15,000 per year, but ROI is increased to 25 percent due to the reduced investment base.

Segment X

	All Other Assets
Gross Book Value	$500,000
Profit	125,000
ROI	25%

The net effect of valuing the asset base at gross book value is generally dysfunctional. The segment manager would be motivated to dispose of Equipment A even if its 15 percent return was above the cost of capital, and even if it were fully depreciated and its net book value was zero.

Replacement Decisions

When assets are replaced, the company must invest an amount equal to the cost of the new asset minus the salvage value of the old asset. However, the use of gross book value as the segment's investment value causes its assets to increase by only the difference between the cost of the new asset (added to the books) and the cost of the old asset (removed from the books). To the segment manager, this means that the additional investment to obtain new assets is quite small, and replacement investments can be made (from the segment manager's perspective) at far less than the cutoff rate used in cash flow models.

For example, if a manager replaces an old asset that cost $35,000 with a new asset that cost $45,000, the increase in the gross book value of the investment base is only $10,000 (old investment base + $45,000 − $35,000 = new investment base). The increase is the same here whether the old asset is relatively new or completely depreciated, because it is the *gross* book value of the old machine that is counted in the investment base.

If segment earnings then increase by $2,000, the additional investment appears to earn a return of 20 percent ($2,000/$10,000). However, if the old asset was worth only $5,000 as a trade-in, the cash investment required is actually $40,000, and the average return only 5 percent ($2,000/$40,000).

ROI of the additional investment, based on the out-of-pocket cost of the investment, is calculated as follows.

Cost of new asset	$45,000
Trade-in (salvage) of old asset	5,000
Cash cost of new asset	$40,000
Increased return	2,000
ROI based on additional investment	5%

ROI of the additional investment, based on the increase in gross book value, is calculated as follows.

Cost of new asset	$45,000
Cost of old asset	35,000
Increase in gross book value	$10,000
Increased return	2,000
ROI based on increased gross value	20%

These calculations are misleading. The cost (to the company) of the new asset is $40,000, but valuing the investment base at gross book value obscures this cost at the segment level and encourages the segment manager to make capital budgeting decisions that are detrimental to the company's best interest. Using gross book value puts the objectives of the segment manager at odds with the objectives of the company as a whole.

Net Book Value

Net book value is the value at which an asset is carried in the accounting records. Net book value is original cost minus any cost already depleted, amortized, or depreciated. For instance, suppose a building cost $500,000 and $100,000 in depreciation expense has been taken on it, yielding a net book value of $400,000. The use of net book value in companies with one asset or assets of a similar age gives a decreasing investment base. This effect is increased when accelerated depreciation methods are used. Because the net book value of an asset is less each year, ROI increases each year. This effect misleads segment managers and may cause them to avoid investing in new assets.

Effect on ROI

Assume that a segment has an investment controllable by the segment manager of $200,000 and net income of $30,000, as follows. ROI is 15 percent ($30,000/$200,000).

Cash	$ 20,000
Inventory	30,000
Equipment	150,000
Total investment in assets	$200,000
Net income	$ 30,000
ROI	15%

Even if the segment keeps exactly the same assets and earns exactly the same profit each year, ROI will not remain 15 percent because the equipment is depreciated each year. Assume the equipment has a life of 5 years and that depreciation expense of $30,000 ($150,000/5 years) is taken each year. Depreciation expense is charged against earnings each year, and the book value of the investment is reduced to zero over the assets' life.

If cash, inventory, and profit remain the same, the net book value of the segment investment and the ROI calculated on the book value is as shown in Exhibit 7–1. ROI is based on net book value at the end of each year, and increases from 17.6 percent at the end of year 1 to 60 percent at the end of year 5, when the equipment is fully depreciated (net book value = zero). The 15 percent ROI occurs only in year 1 and only if the net book value of assets at the beginning of the year is used. By the end of the year, the book value has been decreased by the depreciation expense and ROI has increased.

This effect (an increase in ROI) occurs in companies with only one asset or companies that purchase all their assets in the same year. When a company purchases assets in different years, the distortion is still present but averages out and is not apparent. Additionally, when ROI is calculated using net book value at the beginning of the year, it is different from ROI calculated using book value at the end of the

EXHIBIT 7–1
Increasing ROI Using Net Book Value

End of Year	Assets at Cost	Annual Depreciation	Accumulated Depreciation to Date	Book Value	Profit	ROI (%)
1	$200,000	$30,000	$ 30,000	$170,000	$30,000	17.6
2	200,000	30,000	60,000	140,000	30,000	21.4
3	200,000	30,000	90,000	110,000	30,000	27.3
4	200,000	30,000	120,000	80,000	30,000	37.5
5	200,000	30,000	150,000	50,000	30,000	60.0

year. Some companies attempt to overcome this difference by using the average of beginning and ending book values. In our example, we can calculate the following equally acceptable ROIs for year 1.

Using beginning-of-year
    book value $30,000/$200,000 ROI = 15.0%

Using end-of-year
    book value $30,000/$170,000 ROI = 17.6%

Using average book
    value for the year $30,000/$185,000 ROI = 16.2%

This problem can be avoided by using replacement cost and annuity depreciation. Annuity depreciation uses a mathematical method that results in larger depreciation charges as the asset ages. The method is cumbersome to apply and produces a pattern of depreciation expense that does not match the rate at which assets wear out. Accountants always mention annuity depreciation when discussing the distortion problem, but we know of no company that uses annuity depreciation.

Replacement Cost

Replacement cost is defined several different ways. Assume one segment of a company uses computerized printing equipment that cost $140,000 when purchased five years ago. The equipment has a seven-year life, is depreciated $20,000 per year, and after five years has a net book value of $40,000 [$140,000 − (5 × $20,000)]. The equipment's replacement cost can be estimated using at least three approaches, each leading to a different value.

1. ***Replacement cost as is.*** The cost of replacing the equipment with used equipment in the same condition. If there is no used equipment market and the equipment to be valued is unique, replacement value can be difficult to estimate. Assume used

equipment in the same condition is in demand for use as parts
in repairing old equipment, and costs $60,000.[1]

2. *Replacement cost new.* The cost of replacing the equipment
   with new equipment of exactly the same model and type. Assume the replacement value for the new equipment is $200,000.
   Because the equipment is old, new equipment exactly like the
   old equipment does not exist and requires expensive, custom
   manufacture. Equipment using computer chips two or three
   generations old is frequently no longer manufactured.

3. *Capacity replacement value.* The cost of replacing the capacity
   of the equipment, not the equipment itself, with equipment
   currently manufactured. For computerized equipment, new
   technology often makes it less expensive to purchase the same
   capacity each year. New equipment that can perform the same
   work as the old equipment costs $90,000.

4. *Price-level adjusted historical cost.* Not a true measure of replacement cost. Some companies adjust an asset's cost for
   changes in prices, in order to estimate a current cost. If the
   price index changes from 110 to 165 during the five years the
   company owns the equipment, the price-level adjusted cost of
   the equipment is $140,000 × 165/110 = $210,000.

Even when a definition of replacement cost is chosen, a company
may have great difficulty obtaining annual replacement value estimates
of the myriad assets that make up the factories, stores, and other operating investments of each segment. Estimates by consultants or apprais-
ers are often subjective, and the amounts may vary widely.

---

[1] The amounts in this example are for illustration only.

Economic Value

The economic value of an asset is the present value of the asset's future cash flows. The amount is subjective and difficult to determine. To estimate economic value, managers must first estimate the future cash flows and then decide on an appropriate discount rate. The estimated cash flows must be the flows expected to actually occur, not the flows a manager might target or aspire to. The expected actual cash flows are then discounted to their present value (using the techniques discussed in Chapter 16).

The process produces a conflict between determining the economic value of the investment (based on predictions of a segment manager's performance), and evaluating a segment manager's performance (based on the profit actually generated and the present value of top management's predictions). Performance is, in effect, evaluated against an estimate of itself.

Additionally, the economic value approach gives the same value to an asset, regardless of how it was obtained. If a manager saves money on an equipment acquisition by shopping wisely or building the asset in-house, the manager is assigned the same dollar investment base as another manager who acts foolishly and buys identical equipment at a higher price (assuming the estimated cash flows and discount rate are the same). Because ROI is supposed to improve a segment manager's motivation and top management's evaluation procedures, this valuation method creates serious problems.

To illustrate, assume two retail stores in Kansas City are owned by C. Smith, who wishes to value the assets of the two store managers using the economic value approach. Coincidentally, after deciding that the stores should begin delivering to customers, Smith directs each manager to purchase one delivery truck and to begin delivery service as economically as possible. Smith estimates that the cash flows from the delivery service will be $10,000 per year, and that the trucks will last five years. Smith believes the appropriate discount rate is 10 percent.

One store manager shops wisely and purchases a new truck with the minimum basic equipment for $24,000. The other manager understands the economic value method and buys a top-of-the-line truck, loaded with options, for $40,000. What value is placed on each manager's truck? The present value of $10,000 each year for five years at 10 percent is: $3.791 \times \$10,000 = \$37,910$. Thus, the investment base of each manager is increased by $37,910, the economic value of the truck. A manager who understands this type of valuation is not motivated to find the lowest equipment price.

In practice, managers resist the use of economic value because they do not like to be evaluated with artificial measures concocted by economists. As a result, economic value is not often used to value the investment base in ROI measures.

8

GROSS MARGIN RETURN
ON INVESTMENT

*T*here are several specialized variations of return on investment that managers or investors sometimes use. This chapter and Chapters 9 and 10 discuss variations of ROI that use gross margin, contribution margin, and cash as the measure of investment return. For each return, the investment base must also be suitably modified. Gross margin return on investment (GMROI) attempts to examine the relationship between the gross margin on sales and the investment in inventory required to support the sales. GMROI is gross margin in dollars for a given period divided by the average cost of inventory on hand during the same period. Assume here that the period is one year.

$$\frac{\text{Gross margin}}{\text{Average inventory (at cost)}} = \text{GMROI}$$

The numerator, gross margin, is sales minus the cost of goods (inventory) sold. Sales of $1,000,000 and cost of goods sold of $600,000 yield a gross margin of $400,000. This calculation is often made in the first three lines of the income statement.

Sales	$1,000,000
Cost of goods sold	600,000
Gross margin	$ 400,000

If the $1,000,000 in sales requires an average inventory equal to two months' (one-sixth of a year) cost of sales ($600,000/6) or $100,000, GMROI is 400 percent, or $4 for every $1 invested in inventory.

$$\frac{\text{Gross margin}}{\text{Average inventory (at cost)}} = \text{GMROI}$$

$$\frac{\$400,000}{\$100,000} = 4.00 = 400\%$$

Components of GMROI

Like ROI, GMROI can be broken into margin and turnover components. The margin component of GMROI is the percentage of gross margin on sales. For the example, gross margin on sales is 40 percent.

$$\frac{\text{Gross margin}}{\text{Sales}} = \text{Gross margin on sales}$$

$$\frac{\$400,000}{\$1,000,000} = 0.40 = 40\%$$

The turnover component is inventory turnover, using sales as the numerator. (More commonly, analysts use cost of goods sold, not sales, as the numerator in calculating inventory turnover. Sales is used here and in some published industry ratios.) Inventory turnover in our example is 10.

$$\frac{\text{Sales}}{\text{Inventory}} = \text{Inventory turnover}$$

$$\frac{\$1,000,000}{\$100,000} = 10 \text{ times}$$

Combining these components shows how they interact to give a GMROI of 400 percent. A change in either margin or turnover changes GMROI.

$$\text{Gross margin on sales} \times \text{Inventory turnover} = \text{GMROI}$$

$$\frac{\text{Gross margin}}{\text{Sales}} \times \frac{\text{Sales}}{\text{Inventory}} = \text{GMROI}$$

$$\frac{\$400,000}{\$1,000,000} \times \frac{\$1,000,000}{\$100,000} = \text{GMROI}$$

$$0.40 \times 10 = 4.00 = 400\%$$

Comparing GMROI and ROI

GMROI differs from ROI in two ways: (1) GMROI uses gross margin instead of net income as the return, and (2) GMROI considers only the investment in inventory. Because net income is usually small in relation to a company's total investment in assets, ROI that is calculated using a company's total assets and income is almost always less than 20 percent. But because gross margin is substantially larger than net income, and average inventory is generally much smaller than total assets, GMROI is often quite large relative to ROI.

Managers believe gross margin and the gross margin percentage are important measures. When managers say, for example, "We make a dollar on each shirt sold," they typically mean: "We sell each shirt for a dollar more than its cost." If each shirt costs $2, the selling price is $3, and the gross margin is $1. The gross margin percentage is 33.3 percent, calculated by dividing gross margin by the selling price ($1 ÷ $3).

Net income is determined by subtracting cost of goods sold and all other expenses from sales. The net income created on the sale of each shirt might be only $.20 after the total cost of salespeople, supervision, rent, utilities, and advertising is subtracted from gross margin. Gross margin must be large enough to cover *all* expenses or the company will incur a loss.

Managing GMROI

Managers can improve their GMROI by changing either gross margin or inventory turnover. Gross margin can be increased by either raising the selling price to increase the sales dollars generated from a given cost of goods sold, or by reducing the cost of goods sold without reducing the sales dollars. Turnover can be increased by reducing the average inventory or increasing sales (or taking both actions).

Increasing Gross Margin

For retailers, selling price and the cost of units sold are often set by market forces. A retail store must sell at competitive prices and often must buy its inventory from the same sources that supply its competition. Consequently, a retail store that seeks to change its gross margin must negotiate discounts for buying in large quantities or for buying much of its inventory from the same vendor.

Manufacturers have more opportunities to lower costs than do retailers. Manufacturing costs are composed of raw materials, labor, and overhead. Managers can often lower the cost of manufactured inventory by negotiating lower costs on materials, by automating processes to reduce labor, or by adopting one of the newer manufacturing techniques such as using robotics or just-in-time (JIT) manufacturing. (JIT is a philosophy of eliminating waste developed by Toyota Motor Company after World War II. One approach to eliminating waste stressed in JIT is reducing inventories.)

Continuing the example given earlier in this chapter, GMROI is 400 percent. If management increases the sales dollars by 10 percent (from $1,000,000 to $1,100,000) with no change in volume (cost of goods sold remains $600,000), the gross margin percentage is increased to 0.4545, turnover is increased to 11 times, and GMROI is increased to 500 percent or $5 for every $1 invested in inventory.

$$\frac{\text{Gross margin}}{\text{Sales}} \times \frac{\text{Sales}}{\text{Inventory}} = \text{GMROI}$$

Original performance: $\dfrac{\$400,000}{\$1,000,000} \times \dfrac{\$1,000,000}{\$100,000} = \text{GMROI}$

$$0.40 \quad \times \quad 10 \quad = 4.0 = 400\%$$

Improved performance (10 percent increase in sales dollars): $\dfrac{\$500,000}{\$1,100,000} \times \dfrac{\$1,100,000}{\$100,000} = \text{GMROI}$

$$0.4545 \quad \times \quad 11 \quad = 5.0 = 500\%$$

Increasing Turnover

As the example shows, increasing sales dollars serves a dual purpose: it increases inventory turnover and improves gross margin. Likewise, lower raw material prices or automated processes reduce the per-unit cost of manufactured inventory, which increases both gross margin per unit and inventory turnover. If managers are able to reduce the cost per unit by 5 percent, both inventory on hand and cost of goods sold are decreased by 5 percent. If sales dollars remain at the original level of $1,000,000, and cost of goods sold is reduced by 5 percent to $570,000, gross margin is increased to $430,000. Gross margin percentage is increased to 0.43, turnover is increased to 10.53, and GMROI is increased to 453 percent or $4.53 for every $1 invested in inventory.

	Original Performance	*5 Percent Reduction in Unit Manufacturing Costs*
Sales	$1,000,000	$1,000,000
Cost of goods sold	600,000	570,000
Gross margin	$ 400,000	$ 430,000
Inventory	$ 100,000	$ 95,000

$$\frac{\text{Gross margin}}{\text{Sales}} \times \frac{\text{Sales}}{\text{Inventory}} = \text{GMROI}$$

Improved performance
(5 percent reduction in
unit manufacturing costs)

$$\frac{\$430,000}{\$1,000,000} \times \frac{\$1,000,000}{\$95,000} = \text{GMROI}$$

$$0.43 \quad \times \quad 10.53 \quad = 4.53 = 453\%$$

Just-in time (JIT) and other advanced manufacturing approaches reduce a manufacturer's investment in inventory by reducing both the per-unit manufacturing cost and the time raw materials and partially completed goods are held before being processed. Reducing the length of time inventories are held reduces the average investment in inventories.

To illustrate, our original example assumed that cost of goods sold is $600,000 and the average inventory on hand equals two months' cost of sales ($600,000/12 = $50,000/month × 2 = $100,000). If JIT and other measures allow management to reduce inventory between processes to only one-half of one month's cost of sales ($600,000/12 = $50,000/month × 0.50 = $25,000), turnover is increased to 40, and GMROI to 1600 percent or $16 for each dollar of investment in inventory.

$$\frac{\text{Gross margin}}{\text{Sales}} \times \frac{\text{Sales}}{\text{Inventory}} = \text{GMROI}$$

$$\frac{\$400,000}{\$1,000,000} \times \frac{\$1,000,000}{\$25,000} = \text{GMROI}$$

$$0.40 \quad \times \quad 40 \quad = 16.00 = 1600\%$$

A competitor who does not adopt a JIT approach to manufacturing cannot produce an equivalent GMROI. Assume a competitor who has not adopted JIT has identical sales and still requires two months' cost of sales to remain in inventory. Turnover is still 10 (as in our original calculation), and to generate a GMROI of 1600 percent, the gross margin must be 160 percent. Gross margin would have to be greater than sales, which is impossible.

$$\frac{\text{Gross margin}}{\text{Sales}} \times \frac{\text{Sales}}{\text{Inventory}} = \text{GMROI}$$

$$\frac{?}{\$1,000,000} \times \frac{\$1,000,000}{\$100,000} = \text{GMROI}$$

$$1.60 \quad \times \quad 10 \quad = 16.00 = 1600\%$$

Gross margin percentage must be 160%.

Including Markup in GMROI

Financial ratios are not absolute; the composition of many ratios varies from one analyst to another. Instead of determining inventory turnover with sales as the numerator (as above), we can use cost of goods sold as the numerator and expand the components to include markup. In our original example, markup on cost is 166.7 percent and inventory turnover, using cost of goods sold, is 6 times.

$$\frac{\text{Sales}}{\text{Cost of goods sold}} = \text{Markup on cost}$$

$$\frac{\$1,000,000}{\$600,000} = 1.667 = 166.7\%$$

$$\frac{\text{Cost of goods sold}}{\text{Inventory}} = \text{Inventory turnover}$$

$$\frac{\$600,000}{\$100,000} = 6 \text{ times}$$

Combining these new components shows how they interact to explain a GMROI of 400 percent. GMROI is not changed by using these new components, but a change in any component—margin, markup, or turnover—changes GMROI.

$$\text{Gross margin} \times \text{Markup} \times \text{Inventory turnover} = \text{GMROI}$$

$$\frac{\text{Gross margin}}{\text{Sales}} \times \frac{\text{Sales}}{\text{Cost of goods sold}} \times \frac{\text{Cost of goods sold}}{\text{Inventory}} = \text{GMROI}$$

$$\frac{\$400,000}{\$1,000,000} \times \frac{\$1,000,000}{\$600,000} \times \frac{\$600,000}{\$100,000} = \text{GMROI}$$

$$0.40 \times 1.667 \times 6 = 4.00$$
$$= 400\%$$

Markup is the factor that drives gross margin: higher markup produce higher gross margins. Including markup in the components gives added flexibility to managers trying to increase GMROI. When the relationships are presented in this form, managers see that they can improve GMROI by increasing gross margin, markup, or inventory turnover.

9

CONTRIBUTION MARGIN RETURN ON INVESTMENT

*W*hen making decisions or assessing profitability, many managers avoid gross margin and use contribution margin instead. Contribution margin return on investment (CMROI) is a refinement of gross margin return on investment (GMROI), discussed in Chapter 8. CMROI is often more appropriate for assessing performance or making decisions because it recognizes that costs are not all the same. Unlike gross margin, contribution margin is generally not available to persons outside a company.

Different Types of Costs

When a manufacturer produces more than it sells, thereby increasing the number of units in its inventory, some costs assigned to the increased inventory are "real" costs that require additional current expenditures, and some are not. Additional electricity is consumed, and assemply-line employees work more hours for which they must be paid. These are real cost increases. Allocations (assignments) of costs incurred in prior years, such as depreciation on a plant, or costs that would be spent in the same amount even if production had not increased, such as fire insurance premiums or property taxes, are not-so-real costs that do not require additional current expenditures.

Fixed Costs

Costs that do not change in total when a company's activity level changes are called *fixed costs*. If depreciation on a factory building is

$30,000 per month, it remains $30,000 per month regardless of whether the factory operates one shift or three. If production increases from 10,000 units for one shift to 30,000 units for three shifts, the average depreciation cost per unit decreases from $3 per unit ($30,000/10,000 units) to $1 per unit ($30,000/30,000 units), but the total depreciation cost does not change.

Thus, there is no *incremental (or increased) fixed cost* associated with increased activity. Fixed costs for a manufacturer are generally not the costs of production; they are the costs of maintaining the *capacity* to produce.

Variable Costs

Costs that change in total in direct proportion to changes in a company's activity level are called *variable costs*. Variable costs for a manufacturer include the costs of materials, labor, and some overhead, such as electricity consumed and the maintenance of equipment. If $100 of raw material Z is needed to produce one unit of product, the total cost of raw material Z is $1,000,000 when 10,000 units are produced ($100 × 10,000 units) but $3,000,000 when 30,000 units are produced ($100 × 30,000 units).

Variable costs are *incremental costs* associated with increased activity. The increased cost of producing an additional order is sometimes called the *marginal cost* of producing the order. In our example, the variable cost per unit for raw materials remains the same ($100), but total costs vary directly with activity. The marginal cost of producing an additional 100 units is $10,000 (100 units × $100).

Manufacturing Contribution Margin

CMROI examines the relationship between the contribution margin on sales and the incremental investment in inventory required to support the sales. Contribution margin is calculated by subtracting total variable costs from sales. CMROI uses a contribution margin subtotal, sometimes called manufacturing margin or manufacturing contribution margin, which is calculated by subtracting only variable manufacturing costs (e.g., variable cost of goods sold) from sales. Variable costs of selling and administration, such as commissions or collections, are then subtracted from manufacturing contribution margin to get contribution margin.

Manufacturing contribution margin and contribution margin are calculated as shown in the contribution margin formatted income statement in Exhibit 9–1. Exhibit 9–1 also contains a gross profit formatted or multiple-step income statement. With additions for selling and administrative cost, both income statements contain figures from the main example used throughout Chapter 8.

If $1,000,000 in sales (see Exhibit 9–1) requires an average investment in the variable cost of inventory equal to two months' variable cost of sales ($300,000/12 = $25,000 \times 2) = $50,000, CMROI is 1400 percent, or $14 for every $1 invested in the variable cost of inventory.

$$\frac{\text{Manufacturing contribution margin}}{\text{Average inventory (at variable cost)}} = \text{CMROI}$$

$$\frac{\$700,000}{\$50,000} = 14.00 = 1400\%$$

Two-Component CMROI Analysis

Like ROI or GMROI, CMROI can be broken into two components—margin and turnover. The margin component of CMROI is the manufacturing contribution margin percentage. In our example, manufacturing contribution margin is 70 percent.

$$\frac{\text{Manufacturing CM}}{\text{Sales}} = \frac{\text{Manufacturing contribution}}{\text{margin percentage}}$$

$$\frac{\$700,000}{\$1,000,000} = 0.70 = 70\%$$

EXHIBIT 9–1
Contribution Margin and Gross Profit
Formatted Income Statements

Example Company
Contribution Margin Income Statement
for the Year Ended December 31, 199X

Sales		$1,000,000
Variable cost of goods sold		300,000
Manufacturing contribution margin		700,000
Variable selling costs	$ 50,000	
Variable administrative costs	100,000	150,000
Contribution margin		550,000
Fixed costs:		
Manufacturing	$300,000	
Selling	75,000	
Administrative	25,000	400,000
Net income		$ 150,000

Example Company
Gross Profit Income Statement
for the Year Ended December 31, 199X

Sales		$1,000,000
Cost of goods sold		600,000
Gross profit		400,000
Selling costs	$125,000	
Administrative costs	125,000	250,000
Net income		$ 150,000

As with GMROI, the turnover component is inventory turnover using sales as the numerator, but now only the variable cost of inventory is used as the denominator.

$$\frac{\text{Sales}}{\text{Inventory}} = \text{Inventory turnover}$$

$$\frac{\$1,000,000}{\$50,000} = 20 \text{ times}$$

Manufacturing contribution margin percentage and inventory turnover combine to give the CMROI.

$$\frac{\text{Manufacturing contribution}}{\text{margin percentage}} \quad \times \quad \text{Inventory turnover} \quad = \text{CMROI}$$

$$\frac{\text{Manufacturing contribution margin}}{\text{Sales}} \quad \times \quad \frac{\text{Sales}}{\text{Inventory variable cost}} \quad = \text{CMROI}$$

$$0.70 \quad \times \quad 20 \quad \begin{aligned} &= 14.00 \\ &= 1400\% \end{aligned}$$

Three-Component CMROI Analysis

As with GMROI, CMROI can be broken into three components by calculating inventory turnover using the variable cost of sales (rather than sales). The three components generated are: margin, markup, and turnover. The margin component of CMROI is the manufacturing contribution margin percentage, as calculated previously. Markup and turnover both use variable cost of goods sold.

$$\frac{\text{Sales}}{\text{Variable cost of goods sold}} = \text{Markup}$$

$$\frac{\$1,000,000}{\$300,000} = 3.333 = 333\tfrac{1}{3}\%$$

$$\frac{\text{Variable cost of goods sold}}{\text{Inventory}} = \text{Inventory turnover}$$

$$\frac{\$300,000}{\$50,000} = 6 \text{ times}$$

These three components combine to give the CMROI.

$$\frac{\text{Manufacturing contribution}}{\text{margin percentage}} \quad \times \quad \text{Markup} \quad \times \quad \frac{\text{Inventory}}{\text{turnover}} \quad = \text{CMROI}$$

$$\frac{\text{Manufacturing CM}}{\text{Sales}} \quad \times \quad \frac{\text{Sales}}{\text{Variable cost of goods sold}} \quad \times \quad \frac{\text{Variable cost of goods sold}}{\text{Inventory}} \quad = \text{CMROI}$$

$$0.70 \quad \times \quad 3.333 \quad \times \quad 6 \quad = 14.00$$

Comparing CMROI and GMROI

The excess of sales over variable cost of goods sold is a better measure of the benefit of selling more inventory than the excess of sales over the full cost of goods sold. Likewise, the variable cost of units placed in inventory is a better measure of the investment required to maintain inventory. Because fixed costs do not change in total when inventory is increased or decreased, they are usually irrelevant in decision making and should not be in ratios used to evaluate managerial performance.

Contribution margin impacts income much more directly than gross margin; thus, CMROI is a much more valuable analysis tool than GMROI. Contribution margin can be increased by either raising selling price or lowering variable costs. Decreasing a bookkeeping allocation of fixed costs to cost of goods sold increases GMROI but does not change CMROI. Because bookkeeping allocations of fixed costs do not in any way change total costs, they also do not change CMROI.

10

CASH RETURN
ON INVESTMENT

*I*n a survey of customized measures of return, previous chapters have discussed ROI calculations that use net income, gross profit, and manufacturing contribution margin. This chapter discusses an ROI variation that defines return as cash inflow from operations. Cash inflow is the most rigorous form that a return on investment can take. To stockholders and other investors, income is of high quality only if it is accompanied by an appropriate cash inflow. High-quality earnings are earnings that can be sustained and that are accompanied by appropriate cash inflows.

Low-quality earnings (those not accompanied by cash inflow) result in a lower market value for a company's stock because analysts believe that earnings accompanied by cash inflow are worth more than earnings that are not. Low quality also results when earnings cannot be sustained or when accounting procedures increase earnings without a corresponding increase in cash inflow.

Earnings are not accompanied by sustainable cash flows when managers attempt to increase earnings by changing the timing of revenues and expenses. Managers, for example, might avoid some maintenance procedures to reduce expenses and raise income. If maintenance costing $50,000 is put off until next year, profit in the present year is improved by $50,000 but earnings in the next year are reduced by the same amount. Likewise, managers trying to increase this year's sales by relaxing credit standards may create sales that benefit the current year but are likely to become bad debts in the following year.

Investors downgrade the quality of earnings when a company chooses an accounting method because it maximizes reported earnings. Companies that use straight-line depreciation or FIFO inventory are perceived to have lower-quality earnings than a company that uses an accelerated depreciation method or LIFO inventory.[1] (Companies using straight-line depreciation or FIFO inventory show higher reported earnings relative to companies with the same cash flows that use accelerated depreciation or LIFO inventory.)

Cash ROI

Cash ROI is determined by dividing cash flow from operations during a period by the average investment in total assets during the same period. If average assets are $500,000 and cash flow from operations is $30,000, cash ROI is 6 percent.

$$\frac{\text{Cash flow from operations}}{\text{Average total assets}} = \text{Cash ROI}$$

$$\frac{\$30,000}{\$500,000} = 0.06 = 6\%$$

Like other variations of ROI, the formula for cash ROI has two components—*return on sales* and *turnover*. Return on sales in this case is cash return on sales, and turnover is the turnover of total investment in assets. If sales are $750,000, cash return on sales is 4 percent and asset turnover is 1.5 times.

$$\text{Cash return on sales} \times \text{Asset turnover} = \text{Cash ROI}$$

$$\frac{\text{Cash flow from operations}}{\text{Sales}} \times \frac{\text{Sales}}{\text{Average assets}} = \text{Cash ROI}$$

$$\frac{\$30,000}{\$750,000} \times \frac{\$750,000}{\$500,000} = \text{Cash ROI}$$

$$0.04 \times 1.5 = 0.06 = 6\%$$

---

[1] See Frances L. Ayers, "Perceptions of Earnings Quality: What Managers Need to Know," *Management Accounting,* March 1994, pp. 27–29.

Cash return on sales is a cash flow ratio similar to the profitability ratio, return on sales (i.e., net income/sales). Cash return on sales helps investors evaluate the quality of a company's earnings and determine the extent to which it can support its net income with cash inflow.

The asset turnover ratio measures management's effectiveness in using the company's total assets to generate sales activity. This ratio is discussed in detail in Chapter 2.

Estimating Cash Flow from Operations

Cash flow from operations is shown in every published financial statement. Still, it is common for people to estimate it from net income by adding depreciation and amortization expenses to net income. Cash is consumed when a company purchases an asset such as a plant or a patent, but no cash flows when the cost of the asset is depreciated or amortized against earnings each year. Depreciation and amortization expenses are allocations of an asset's original cost to a period benefited by the asset's use. Because they are allocations, depreciation and amortization are operating expenses that do not require operating cash outflows each year.

Depreciation and amortization are subtracted in the income statement but do not require cash outflows. Thus, many people feel that adding them back to net income provides a good approximation of cash flow from operations. Exhibit 10–1 shows the income statement and statement of cash flows for SCANA Corporation. SCANA's cash flow from operations is estimated by adding its depreciation and amortization to its net income ($119,177,000 + $151,199,000 = $270,376,000). Net cash provided from operating activities is shown as $296,705,000 (Exhibit 10–2).

Although this technique is frequently used, it is inaccurate and unpredictable. In a study of fifty companies, cash from operations was determined (1) by adding depreciation and amortization back into net income, and (2) by reading it from the companies' own statement of

EXHIBIT 10–1
Consolidated Statements of Income and Retained Earnings for SCANA Corporation

For the Years Ended December 31,	1994	1993	1992
	(Thousands of Dollars except per share amounts)		
Operating Revenues (Notes 1 and 2):			
Electric	$ 975,388	$ 940,121	$ 829,477
Gas	342,672	320,195	305,275
Transit	4,002	3,851	3,623
Total operating revenues	1,322,062	1,264,167	1,138,375
Operating Expenses:			
Fuel used in electric generation	235,136	229,736	206,151
Purchased power	20,104	13,057	7,323
Gas purchased for resale	220,923	208,695	191,577
Other operation (Note 1)	229,996	223,239	215,800
Maintenance (Note 1)	63,725	67,652	65,442
Depreciation and amortization (Note 1)	119,177	112,844	108,315
Income taxes (Notes 1 and 7)	94,510	90,007	60,947
Other taxes	78,938	73,626	73,040
Total operating expenses	1,062,509	1,018,856	928,595
Operating Income	259,553	245,311	209,780
Other Income (Note 1):			
Other income (loss), net of income taxes	(2,178)	21,147	6,388
Allowance for equity funds used during construction	8,176	8,929	5,495
Total other income	5,998	30,076	11,883
Income Before Interest Charges and Preferred Stock Dividends	265,551	275,387	221,663
Interest Charges (Credits):			
Interest on long-term debt, net	108,804	98,695	93,052
Other interest expense	6,749	8,672	8,819
Allowance for borrowed funds used during construction (Note 1)	(7,156)	(6,178)	(4,271)
Total interest charges, net	108,397	101,189	97,600
Income Before Preferred Stock Cash Dividends of Subsidiary	157,154	174,198	124,063
Preferred Stock Cash Dividends of Subsidiary (At stated rates)	(5,955)	(6,217)	(6,473)
Net Income	151,199	167,981	117,590
Retained Earnings at Beginning of Year	506,380	462,893	457,393
Common Stock Cash Dividends Declared (Note 5)	(133,911)	(124,494)	(112,090)
Retained Earnings at End of Year	$ 523,668	$ 506,380	$ 462,893
Net Income	$ 151,199	$ 167,981	$ 117,590
Weighted Average Number of Common Shares Outstanding (Thousands)	47,381	45,203	41,475
Earnings per Weighted Average Share of Common Stock	$3.19	$3.72	$2.84

EXHIBIT 10–2
Consolidated Statements of Cash Flows for SCANA Corporation

For the Years Ended December 31,	1994	1993	1992
	(Thousands of Dollars)		
Cash Flows from Operating Activities:			
Net income	$151,199	$167,981	$117,590
Adjustments to reconcile net income to net cash provided from operating activities:			
Depreciation, depletion and amortization	210,905	158,024	126,695
Amortization of nuclear fuel	13,487	18,156	23,190
Deferred income taxes, net	9,967	65,205	(10,783)
Deferred investment tax credits, net	(3,632)	(3,658)	(3,667)
Net regulatory asset—accumulated deferred income taxes	(1,951)	(31,531)	—
Dividends declared on preferred stock of subsidiary	5,955	6,217	6,473
Allowance for funds used during construction	(15,332)	(15,107)	(9,766)
Unamortized loss on reacquired debt	(60)	(17,063)	(81)
Nuclear refueling accrual	(4,881)	(6,086)	11,862
Equity in (earnings) losses of investees	(230)	(319)	652
Over (under) collections, fuel adjustment clause	(16,966)	(14,308)	7,482
Emission allowances	(19,409)	—	—
Changes in certain current assets and liabilities:			
(Increase) decrease in receivables	(9,059)	(35,244)	(8,918)
(Increase) decrease in inventories	2,131	(10,995)	(234)
Increase (decrease) in accounts payable	(11,536)	28,109	7,282
Increase (decrease) in estimated rate refunds and related interest	(2,509)	(15,302)	17,811
Increase (decrease) in taxes accrued	(3,393)	(14,941)	1,691
Increase (decrease) in interest accrued	3,442	(7,511)	663
Other, net	(11,423)	3,955	12,354
Net Cash Provided from Operating Activities	296,705	275,582	300,296
Cash Flows from Investing Activities:			
Utility property additions and construction expenditures	(404,600)	(322,381)	(277,636)
(Increase) decrease in nonutility property and investments:			
Acquisitions of oil and gas producing properties	(47,189)	(122,621)	(74,766)
Nonutility property	(109,336)	(81,044)	(35,462)
Investments	(19,006)	(4,066)	(2,591)
Sale of real estate assets	79,439	—	—
Principal noncash item:			
Allowance for funds used during construction	15,332	15,107	9,766
Net Cash Used for Investing Activities	(485,360)	(515,005)	(380,689)

(continued)

EXHIBIT 10–2 (continued)

For the Years Ended December 31,	1994	1993	1992
	(Thousands of Dollars)		
Cash Flows from Financing Activities:			
Proceeds:			
Issuance of mortgage bonds	100,000	600,000	—
Issuance of common stock	63,317	129,066	126,809
Issuance of notes and loans	60,000	148,059	154,254
Issuance of pollution control bonds	30,000	—	—
Other long-term debt	—	3,005	—
Repayments:			
Mortgage bonds	—	(430,000)	(35,890)
Notes	(75,545)	(72,040)	(95,272)
Other long-term debt	(11,430)	(1,195)	(255)
Preferred stock	(3,398)	(3,295)	(3,199)
Dividend payments:			
Common stock	(131,925)	(122,129)	(109,383)
Preferred stock	(6,048)	(6,247)	(6,558)
Short-term borrowings, net	140,008	1,863	20,390
Fuel financings, net	13,844	(18,948)	(6,628)
Net Cash Provided by Financing Activities	178,823	228,139	44,268
Net Decrease in Cash and Temporary Cash Investments	(9,832)	(11,284)	(36,125)
Cash and Temporary Cash Investments, January 1	20,766	32,050	68,175
Cash and Temporary Cash Investments, December 31	$ 10,934	$ 20,766	$ 32,050
Supplemental Cash Flows Information:			
Cash paid for—Interest	$110,347	$113,010	$100,340
—Income taxes	90,012	93,337	81,819
Noncash Financing Activities:			
Department of Energy decontamination and decommissioning obligation	—	4,965	—

cash flows. We found that half of the estimates were too high, and half were too low. Cash flow from operations, estimated from net income for our sample, was in error by an average difference of 92.28 percent.

Operating Cash Flows

Cash flow from operations is shown in a statement of cash flows published in a company's annual report. The statement of cash flows shows cash flow, in or out, for three separate activities: (1) operating, (2) financing, and (3) investing. The direct method or the indirect method may be used in the statement of cash flows to determine and present cash flow from operating activities.

The Direct Method

The direct method of determining and presenting cash flow is essentially a cash-basis income statement. Operating cash flows are separated into major categories of receipts and payments, and their net amount is the cash flow provided by or used in operations. There is no cash flow for depreciation or amortization, so these expenses are not used in determining cash flow from operations using the direct method. Likewise, the amount of a gain or loss shown in an income statement does not show the amount or direction of any related cash flow. Land that cost $9,000 and is sold for $7,000 produces a loss of $2,000 but a cash inflow of $7,000. Because a sale of land is not an operating activity, the $7,000 inflow would appear as an investing activity cash inflow, a separate category appearing below cash from operations in a statement of cash flows.

The general form of the direct method is shown in Exhibit 10–3.

EXHIBIT 10–3
Operating Cash Flows Using the Direct Method

ABC Company
Scheduling of Operating Cash Flows
for the Year Ended December 31, 199X

Cash collected from customers		$50,000
Less cash paid for expenses:		
Goods sold	$20,000	
Salaries and wages	15,000	
Other operating costs	10,000	45,000
Net cash provided by operating activities		$ 5,000

The Indirect Method

The indirect method of preparing and presenting cash flow from operations in the statement of cash flows does not determine the major categories of operating cash flows. The indirect method adjusts net income up or down for differences between revenues and expenses, and the actual cash flows from operations. Differences between the income statement amounts and the related operating cash flows result in changes in the current asset and liability accounts, because, for the most part, each of these accounts is linked directly to an operating revenue or expense. (Inventory and accounts payable, for example, are linked to cost of goods sold, and accounts receivable are linked to sales revenue.) Cash provided by operations is calculated by (1) adding to net income any changes in current asset or liability accounts that result in increases in cash from operations, and (2) subtracting from net income any changes that result in decreases in cash from operations. Changes in the current accounts affect cash flow as shown in the following summary.

Change in Account	Effect on Cash from Operations	Add (Subtract) to (from) Net Income (NI) to Determine Cash from Operations
Increase in current asset	Decrease in cash	Subtract from NI
Decrease in current asset	Increase in cash	Add to NI
Increase in current liability	Increase in cash	Add to NI
Decrease in current liability	Decrease in cash	Subtract from NI

Again, because depreciation and amortization expenses do not affect cash flow, they are added back to net income. For the same reason, any losses (or gains) are also adjustments added to (or subtracted from) net income.

EXHIBIT 10–4
Operating Cash Flows Using the Indirect Method

ABC Company
Scheduling of Operating Cash Flows
for the Year Ended December 31, 199X

Net income for 199X		$ 1,000
Plus:		
Depreciation	$3,000	
Loss on sale of equipment	1,000	
Increase in wages payable	2,000	
Decrease in accounts receivable	1,000	7,000
Less:		
Increase in inventory	2,000	
Decrease in accounts payable	1,000	(3,000)
Net cash provided by operating activities		$5,000

Exhibit 10–3 shows the format for the indirect method of determining cash flow from operations for ABC Company. (The SCANA statement of cash flows in Exhibit 10–4 uses the indirect method to calculate cash from operations.)

11

ANALYZING
SALES REVENUES

*M*anagers often differ in the number of profit components they control. Investment center managers control either a whole company or a segment of a company that operates as an autonomous unit, having both profit and an underlying asset investment base. Profit center managers are responsible for maximizing profits but not for managing the asset base. Revenue center managers control only sales or some other revenue-generating activity and are not responsible for either the costs incurred or the investment base used.

As part (or all) of their duties, investment, profit, revenue center managers contribute to the profitability of a company and to ROI by increasing revenue production. Analyzing revenue production involves more than simply looking at the total dollars of revenue generated. Analysis of changes in the market, variations from budget for total revenues, and any changes from budget in the percentage of customer accounts collected also provides useful information.

Market Size Variance

If the market for a company's products changes, sales revenue may decrease despite good performance by a revenue or profit center manager. Any analysis of revenue generation where a company has a substantial market share (perhaps 5 percent or more) should include a determination of the effect of changes in market size.

For example, assume the manager of wholesale refrigerator sales in Chicago is responsible only for the total refrigerator sales revenues generated. The home office in Minneapolis is responsible for all facilities, advertising, and other costs. In preparing sales forecasts for the year, the manager establishes a target for Chicago: 10,000 refrigerators at a standard price of $400 each. The manager actually sells only 8,000 refrigerators during the year, creating a 2,000–unit variance. At the standard selling price, this creates an $800,000 unfavorable (UF) variance from forecasted sales.

Forecasted sales	10,000	refrigerators
Actual sales	(8,000)	refrigerators
Market variance	2,000	refrigerators UF
	× $400	standard price/refrigerator
	$800,000	UF

To analyze the manager's performance in a meaningful way, we must first look at the expected (forecasted) market for refrigerators in Chicago and the market that actually existed.

Forecasted market	100,000	refrigerators
Actual market	(90,000)	refrigerators
Market variance	10,000	refrigerators UF

From these data, we can view the manager's forecast not as 10,000 refrigerators, but as sales of 10 percent of the Chicago refrigerator market (0.10 × 100,000 refrigerators = 10,000 refrigerators). Viewed this way, 1,000 units or $400,000 (1,000 refrigerators × $400 standard price) of the manager's unfavorable variance is due to environmental influences the manager could not control.

Number of Refrigerators

	Market	Sales at 10% of Market
Forecast	100,000	10,000
Market variance	(10,000) UF	(1,000) UF
Actual market	90,000	
Adjusted sales forecast		9,000

The manager's performance must be evaluated in relation to the total revenue available. A decline in the size of the refrigerator market is beyond the manager's control.

Market Share Variance

Once we have corrected for a variance in the size of the market and its effect on the manager's forecast, we can determine whether the manager achieved the targeted market share. After adjusting the target, the manager expected to sell 9,000 refrigerators but sold only 8,000. The manager's market share has declined by 2.22 percent.

Forecasted market share	10,000/100,000 refrigerators = 10.00%
Less: Actual market share	8,000/90,000 refrigerators = 8.88%
Market share variance	= 2.22% UF

In units and dollars, the market variance and market share variance are shown as follows:

	Market	Sales at 10% of Market	
Forecast	100,000	10,000	refrigerators
Market variance	(10,000)	(1,000)	refrigerators UF
Actual market	90,000	9,000	refrigerators
Actual sales		(8,000)	refrigerators
Market share variance		1,000	refrigerators UF
		× $400	standard price/refrigerator
		$400,000	UF

	In Units		At Standard Price
	Market	Sales at 10% of Market	Sales at $400 Standard/Unit
Forecast	100,000	10,000	$4,000,000
Market variance	(10,000) UF	(1,000) UF	(400,000) UF
Actual market	90,000		
Adjusted forecast		9,000	3,600,000
Actual sales		(8,000)	(3,200,000)
Market share variance		1,000 UF	$ 400,000 UF

Managers should be held responsible only for the variances they can control. The difference between the manager's target sales quantity and actual sales quantity is summarized as follows:

	Units	Sales Dollars at Standard Price
Forecast	10,000	$4,000,000
Market variance	(1,000) UF	(400,000) UF
Market share variance	(1,000) UF	(400,000) UF
Actual sales	8,000	$3,200,000

Sales Volume Variances and Profits

When managers increase or decrease sales revenue by changing the number of units sold, there is a corresponding change in the cost of goods sold and perhaps other expenses, such as commissions or product delivery costs. (Fixed expenses such as insurance or managers' salaries do not change.) Thus, revenues change in direct proportion to a change in units (selling half as many units results in half as much revenue), but *total* expenses, and hence profits, do not. Because of this, differences between actual sales and budgeted sales

116

that result from volume differences (not selling price differences) are often stated in terms of their impact on profits.

If a refrigerator with a standard selling price of $400 has a budgeted cost of $250, the effect on the budgeted profit of each unit change in sales volume is $150 ($400 − $250), the amount each unit contributes to profit. For simplicity, assume that all of the costs that change as a result of a change in sales activity (e.g., cost of units, bad debts, commissions, or advertising) are contained in the $250 budgeted cost per unit, here called "cost of sales and other at budgeted cost." Also assume that all costs that do not change as a result of changes in sales (e.g., insurance or managers' salaries) are contained in the $400,000 "other expenses not changing with sales" category. With these assumptions, the company budgets a profit of $1,100,000 for the Chicago area.

Budgeted Income for Chicago at Budgeted Sales Quantity

Sales at standard cost (10,000 × $400)	$4,000,000
Cost of sales and other at budgeted cost (10,000 × $250)	2,500,000
Budgeted gross margin	1,500,000
Other expenses not changing with sales volume	400,000
Budgeted net income	$1,100,000

If we change the budgeted sales quantity to the actual sales quantity of 8,000 units, while keeping the standard selling price at $400, the budgeted cost per unit at $250, and "other expenses . . ." at $400,000, we find income decreases by $300,000. (This result is not unexpected. We know that each unit sold is budgeted to contribute $150 to profit, and 10,000 − 8,000 = 2,000 units × $150 = $300,000.)

Budgeted Income for Chicago at Actual Sales Quantity

Sales at standard cost (8,000 × $400)	$3,200,000
Cost of sales and other at budgeted cost (8,000 × $250)	2,000,000
Budgeted gross margin	1,200,000
Other expenses not changing with sales volume	400,000
Budgeted net income	$ 800,000

Working from these income statements, our analysis of volume changes due to market and market share variances explains the change in profit, as follows.

	Units	Profit per Unit	Total Profit in Dollars
Forecast profit			$1,100,000
Market variance	(1,000) UF	× $150	(150,000) UF
Market share variance	(1,000) UF	× $150	(150,000) UF
Profit after market variances			$ 800,000

Sales Price Variances

When there is a change in the selling price per unit of a company's products, the increase or decrease goes directly to the bottom line because there is no accompanying change in cost. If the manager in our example actually sold 8,000 refrigerators at $420 (rather than at the forecasted price of $400), the $20 increase in selling price per unit results in a $20 per unit increase in profit. The variance due to the change in selling price is $160,000 favorable (F):

$$8,000 \text{ units} \times \$20/\text{unit increase in selling price} = \$160,000 \text{ F}$$

At an actual selling price of $420/unit and an actual volume of 8,000 units, total sales revenues are $3,360,000 (8,000 units × $420) and the difference between the manager's forecasted sales and actual sales performance is now summarized as follows. (Notice that each of the variances is shown as it alone affects sales, and that actual sales contains the effect of all three variances.)

118

	Units	Standard Price per Unit	Sales Dollars	
Market share variance	(10,000) UF	× $400	$(4,000,000) UF	
Forecast sales	10,000	× $400	$4,000,000	
Sales volume variances:				
Market variance	(1,000) UF	× 400	(400,000) UF	
Market share variance	(1,000) UF	× 400	(400,000) UF	
			3,200,000	
Sales price variance	8,000	× 20	160,000	F
Actual sales	8,000	× 420	$3,360,000	

When the actual selling price is $420/unit, the effect on budgeted profit of the market, market share, and sales price variances is shown as follows.

	Units	Standard Profit per Unit	Profit in Dollars	
Forecast profit	10,000	NA	$1,100,000	
Sales volume variances:				
Market variance	(1,000) UF	× $150	(150,000) UF	
Market share variance	(1,000) UF	× 150	(150,000) UF	
Sales price variance	8,000	× 20	160,000	F
Actual profit			$ 960,000	

Sales Collection Variance

Chapter 10 discusses cash ROI and points out that, to be viewed by investors as having high quality, earnings must be accompanied by cash flows. Cash flows from sales are often determined by the company's ability to collect credit sales. If the company fails to screen customers properly or to anticipate economic downturns, sales could result in uncollectible accounts expense rather than cash inflows.

Thus, it is useful to reconcile budgeted cash collections from sales to actual cash collected from sales. If collection is a problem, the sales collection variance should be determined and isolated. Collections are as important as sales volume or selling price.

Assume the company in our example sells on credit and budgets uncollectible sales of 6 percent of total sales. Due to a change in credit policy, the company actually has uncollectible sales of 10 percent—four percentage points higher than forecasted—and the sales collection variance is 4 percent of $3,360,000, or $134,400 UF.

An analysis of the difference between actual and budgeted performance, including a consideration of the cash collection variance, follows.

	Units	Sales Dollars
Forecasted sales	10,000	$4,000,000
Sales volume variances:		
Market variance	(1,000) UF	(400,000) UF
Market share variance	(1,000) UF	(400,000) UF
Sales price variance	NA	160,000 F
Actual sales	8,000	3,360,000
Less: Budgeted uncollectible sales (6%)		(201,600)
Budgeted cash collections from sales		$3,158,400
Less: Collection variance (4%)		(134,400) UF
Actual cash collected from sales (90%)		$3,024,000

Budgeted uncollectible accounts expense is included in determining the company's forecasted profit. The collection variance is actually a variance in uncollectible accounts expense. Changes in uncollectible accounts expense (collection variance) are included in the following reconciliation of budgeted and actual profits.

	Units	Profit in Dollars
Forecasted profit		$1,100,000
Sales volume variances:		
Market variance	(1,000) UF	(150,000) UF
Market share variance	(1,000) UF	(150,000) UF
Sales price variance		160,000 F
Actual profit before collection variance		$ 960,000
Collection variance		(134,400) UF
Actual profit		$ 825,600

Summary Analysis

The manager in our example forecasted sales of 10 percent of the Chicago refrigerator market, to consist of 10,000 refrigerators sold for a standard price of $400 each, or total sales of $4,000,000. The manager's actual profit for the year is $825,600 on sales of $3,360,000. Profit is $274,400 less than target, and sales are off by $640,000 ($400,000 + $400,000 − $160,000).

Let's analyze the manager's performance. The Chicago market was 10 percent less than forecasted, and the manager lost 10 percent of the company's predicted unit market share. The combined effect of these losses reduced sales by $800,000 and profit by $300,000. In response to slow profit growth, the manager increased selling price to an average of $420 per unit for the year, and loosened credit terms. Some of the lost sales dollars were recovered by raising the selling price. Profit increased by $160,000 as a result of the price change but fell $134,400 because of higher uncollectibles resulting from the new credit policies.

Variances from the budgeted $250 per unit, or the budgeted $400,000 in other expenses could exist, but the Chicago manager is responsible only for sales revenues.

Using the budgeted cost of sales and other expenses, but the actual quantity, price, and collection rate that were controllable by the Chicago manager, the income performance for Chicago is as follows.

Sales (8,000 × $420)	$3,360,000
Cost of sales and other at budgeted cost (8,000 × $250)	2,000,000
Budgeted gross margin	1,360,000
Additional uncollectible accounts expense[1]	134,400
Other expenses not changing with sales (budgeted)	400,000
Net income	$ 825,600

---

[1] Because of our beginning assumptions, the budgeted 6 percent uncollectible accounts expense must be included in the $250/unit "cost of sales and other at budgeted cost." Only the 4 percent additional amount is shown as additional uncollectible accounts expense.

12

ANALYZING COSTS

*I*n the previous chapter, we looked at techniques used to analyze variances in return caused by revenues that are different from a targeted or budgeted level. This chapter discusses variances in return that result from costs that are different from budget. The variances in these two chapters are used as the starting point for detailed analysis of variations in profit and ROI.

Variable Costs

For costs that are expected to vary, in total, in direct proportion with activity, all price and quantity variances are calculated in the same way. These costs are called variable costs—for example, the cost of energy, raw materials, supplies, maintenance, and assembly-line labor.

Exhibit 12–1 is a graph of a typical variable cost. The activity involved is packaging an item sold for delivery. Each packaging activity unit requires $1.50 in raw material.

Variable Cost Standards

Variable cost budgets for departments or projects are generally prepared by first budgeting the cost of each component activity of the department or project. A budget for the cost of payroll department begins with budgets for such items as the cost of authorizing and printing one check, and the marginal (or additional) cost of typing and mailing one letter. Total budgeted payroll department costs then are determined as the total of: 52 weekly payrolls consisting of 1,000

EXHIBIT 12–1
Graph of a Variable Cost
(Packaging Merchandise for Delivery to Customers)

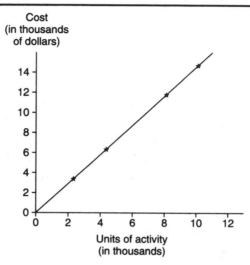

checks at an average of $60 per check, plus 36,000 letters per year at a budgeted cost of $5 per letter, plus budgeted annual amounts for the costs of other activities.

The cost of each activity that has a separate amount in the budget is often called a "standard cost." Thus, we speak of the standard cost of printing a weekly payroll check, or the standard cost per letter typed and mailed. Whatever the activity, its total standard cost is determined from the standard (or budgeted) quantity of an input allowed for a unit and the standard (or budgeted) cost of the input.

$$\text{Standard quantity of inputs} \times \text{Standard price of inputs} = \text{Standard cost of output}$$

Variances from Budgeted Cost

Mathematically, only two things can cause a variance between budgeted or standard variable cost and the actual cost incurred: (1) a difference between budgeted quantity (e.g., number of payrolls or number of letters typed) and actual quantity of inputs, or (2) a difference between standard and the actual cost of the inputs. Consider, for example, the standard for letters typed and mailed.

$$\begin{array}{c} \text{Budgeted quantity} \\ \text{of inputs} \end{array} \times \begin{array}{c} \text{Standard price} \\ \text{of inputs} \end{array} = \text{Budgeted cost of output}$$

$$36{,}000 \text{ letters} \quad \times \quad \$5/\text{letter} \quad = \$180{,}000$$

The actual total cost will be different from budget if the quantity of letters typed is different—say, 38,000 letters instead of the budgeted 36,000.

$$\begin{array}{c} \text{Actual quantity} \\ \text{of inputs} \end{array} \times \begin{array}{c} \text{Standard price} \\ \text{of inputs} \end{array} = \begin{array}{c} \text{Standard cost} \\ \text{of actual output} \end{array}$$

$$38{,}000 \text{ letters} \quad \times \quad \$5/\text{letter} \quad = \quad \$190{,}000$$

The quantity variance is $10,000 unfavorable ($190,000 − $180,000). An alternate way to calculate a quantity variance follows.

Change in quantity of inputs × Standard price of inputs = Quantity variance
2,000 additional letters   × $5/letter   = $10,000 unfavorable

Actual results also differ from budget if cost varies from the amount allowed by the standard. Assume the administration department not only types 2,000 more letters than expected, but also pays $6 per letter typed, rather than the budgeted $5 price.

$$\begin{array}{c} \text{Actual quantity} \\ \text{of inputs} \end{array} \times \begin{array}{c} \text{Actual price} \\ \text{of inputs} \end{array} = \begin{array}{c} \text{Actual cost} \\ \text{of actual output} \end{array}$$

$$38{,}000 \text{ letters typed} \times \quad \$6/\text{letter} \quad = \quad \$228{,}000$$

The price variance is $38,000 unfavorable ($228,000 − $190,000). An alternate way to calculate a price variance follows.

Actual quantity of inputs × Actual price of inputs =   Price variance
38,000 letters   × $1/letter unfavorable = $38,000 unfavorable

When 38,000 letters are typed at an actual cost of $6/letter, the total variance is $48,000 unfavorable.

Price variance	$38,000 unfavorable
Quantity variance	10,000 unfavorable
Total variance	$48,000 unfavorable

Same Variances, Different Names

Although price and quantity variances for all variable costs are calculated in the same manner, they are often called by different names. Price variances are sometimes called rate variances or spending variances. Quantity variances can be called efficiency variances or usage variances. Here are some examples of general usage.

- A difference in the hourly wage of an assembly-line worker is a rate variance.

- A difference in the cost of supplies is a spending variance.

- A difference in the number of labor hours worked is an efficiency variance.

- A difference in the quantity of raw materials used is a usage variance.

When standards are set at realistic levels, favorable variances (1) signal that operations are efficient and effective, and (2) result in lower costs and increased net income. Unfavorable variances (1) indicate that operations are inefficient and ineffective, and (2) increase costs and reduce net income.

Investigating Variances

Separating a variance into its price and quantity components does not tell a manager why the variance occurred. After the manager calculates price and quantity variances, further investigation is needed to see why the variances occurred. In our example, the actual cost per letter might increase because of a change in the cost of paper or postage. The $5 standard may have been inaccurate or out-of-date. The number of letters might increase because the number of employees, customers, or vendors with whom the company corresponds has increased. Or, management may decide to improve relations by increasing its communications with one of these groups.

Alternately, an increase in computerization or the use of form letters might lower the cost per letter. Increased use of electronic mail (e-mail) might reduce the number of letters. Exhibit 12–2 lists a few of the causes a manager might encounter for variances in correspondence costs.

EXHIBIT 12–2
Payroll Department: Reasons for
Cost Variances in Processing Correspondence

Price variances may result from:
- Changes in postage.
- Changes in the cost of printing stationery or envelopes.
- Changes in the specified quality of stationery or envelopes.
- Changes in the wages of typists or other workers involved.
- Changes in the level of skill specified in job descriptions for typist or other personnel.
- Turnover in the department.
- Hiring of part-time help.
- Changes in the level of computerization.
- Aging of equipment.

Quantity variances may result from:
- Changes in the number of employees or others receiving correspondence.
- Increased use of e-mail.
- Changes in policy.
- Changes in the use of bulletin boards.
- Changes in the company environment requiring communication to workers.
- New management styles.

A variance in one department is sometimes causes by poor work done in another department. If, for instance, an employee in the purchasing department buys low-quality envelopes at a price below the purchasing budget, a favorable price variance will be generated in the purchasing department. However, if the envelopes have a poor quality glue, they may stick to each other or fail to seal. Any difficulty using the less expensive, low-quality envelopes might increase the cost to process each letter.

Fixed Cost Variances

Fixed costs are expenses that do not vary, in total, with changes in activity. A fixed cost remains constant in total, despite changes in operating activity. Among a company's typical fixed costs are: fire insurance premiums, property taxes on a building, lease payments for equipment, and monthly compensation of all salaried workers. Exhibit 12–3 shows the graph of a typical fixed cost—leasing of equipment at an annual cost of $10,000.

It is relatively easy to estimate the amount of per unit and total variable cost at any level of activity: increase activity by 10 (or 100 or 1,000) units, and the total variable costs will increase by 10 (or 100 or 1,000) times the variable cost per unit. For example, if we increase the number of letters typed by 10, the total cost increases by $60 (10 × $6). Dividing the $60 increase by the 10-letter increase in quantity gives us the earlier variable cost of $6/letter. The cost per unit of a variable cost does not change in response to changes in activity.

Determining a total and per-unit amount for fixed costs is more difficult because total fixed costs do not change when activity is changed. The payroll department manager's salary—say, $50,000—is the same at 36,000 letters as it is at 38,000 letters. What changes, each time total activity changes, is the fixed cost per unit of activity, as illustrated in Exhibit 12–4. (For example purposes, we make the

EXHIBIT 12–3
Graph of a Fixed Cost
(Leased Equipment)

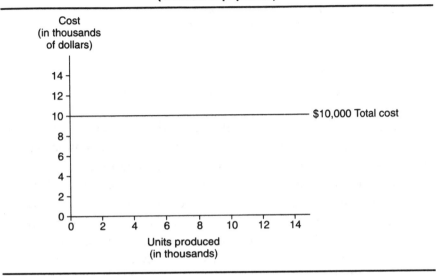

Cost
(in thousands
of dollars)

14
12
10 ———————————————— $10,000 Total cost
8
6
4
2
0

0   2   4   6   8   10   12   14

Units produced
(in thousands)

EXHIBIT 12–4
Graph of Manager's Salary

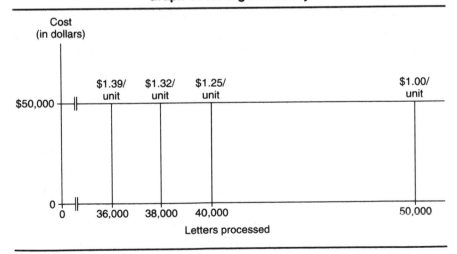

Cost
(in dollars)

$1.39/ $1.32/ $1.25/ $1.00/
unit   unit   unit   unit

$50,000

0

0   36,000   38,000   40,000   50,000

Letters processed

unrealistic assumption that the manager's entire salary, a fixed cost, relates to letters processed.)

$50,000 Salary Divided by		*Cost per Letter*
36,000 letters	=	$1.39
38,000 letters	=	$1.32
40,000 letters	=	$1.25
50,000 letters	=	$1.00

Because fixed costs are not linked directly to specific activities as variable costs are, fixed costs must be costed (assigned or allocated) to units of activity in an arbitrary way. If, at the beginning of the year, the budget for the payroll department includes a $50,000 salary for the department manager, the cost per letter or check can be determined only arbitrarily. Because the manager's salary pays not only for managing correspondence, but also for preparing checks and perhaps performing other activities, we must first divide the salary among those areas. How much of the manager's salary should be allocated to letters? To checks? To other activities?

A consultant may observe the manager over a period of time and determine that 20 percent of the manager's time is devoted to supporting letter writing and processing, 30 percent goes to weekly payrolls, and 50 percent is spent on various other activities, such as the preparation of checks for salaried personnel. Using the previously budgeted activity levels of 36,000 letters annually and 1,000 checks each week (5,200 per year), per-unit amounts are as follows.

Letter writing and processing. $50,000 × 0.20 = $10,000 divided by 36,000 letters = $0.28 salary/letter

Payroll check preparation. $50,000 × 0.30 = $15,000 divided by 52,000 checks = $.288 salary/check

(Other activities are assigned the remaining $25,000 [$50,000 × 0.50])

The salary/unit amounts we calculated are volume-specific. If the company started a second shift, adding another 100 workers, the cost per unit would change, even though the manager's salary stayed the same. Likewise, the percentage of the manager's time necessary to process the weekly payroll might increase only a small amount, because the manager is responsible for managing the check-writing process, not creating the checks. In all likelihood, at 2,000 checks per week, the manager's salary per check would simply be half what it was at 1,000.

These unit costs are all arbitrary. Suppose a second consultant divides the manager's salary not by time but by the importance of the activity in the manager's job description, and apportions 5 percent for correspondence, 50 percent for weekly payrolls, and 45 percent to other responsibilities. If we recalculate the per-unit costs budgeted for 36,000 letters and 52,000 checks, we get completely different amounts. The choice is arbitrary.

$50,000 × 0.05 = $2,500 divided by 36,000 letters = $0.07 salary/letter

$50,000 × 0.05 = $25,000 divided by 52,000 checks = $.481 salary/check

(Other activities are assigned the remaining $22,500 [$50,000 × 0.45])

Fixed Cost Budget Variance

When a manager actually incurs a different total amount than was budgeted for a fixed cost, the manager has an unfavorable or favorable budget variance. Favorable budget variances are generally signs of efficient, effective cost management and increases in net income; unfavorable budget variances, conversely, are indicative of inefficient, ineffective cost management and reduced net income.

If property taxes are budgeted at $10,000 but, due to an unexpected vote in the legislature, are increased to an actual cost of $12,000, the company has an unfavorable budget variance of $2,000.

Budgeted cost	$10,000
Actual cost	12,000
Budget variance	$ 2,000 unfavorable

Managers must find and, if possible, remedy the causes of unfavorable fixed cost variances. In the case of an increase in property taxes, the manager cannot avoid the variance.

Setting Standards

Managers sometimes set standards based on past results, perhaps adjusted for inflation or a change in operating methods. Using historical results to set standards tends to perpetuate the inefficiencies of the past by incorporating them into expectations about the future.

Time-and-motion studies and other engineering methods are frequently used to set labor standards. Engineers may also set equipment maintenance standards or establish specifications for materials in a manufacturing operation. Such approaches do not use historical data but may set standards using unattainable engineering ideals.

Perhaps the best method for setting standards is to use the judgment of the managers who must meet the standards, by introducing a participative standard-setting process. This cooperative effort may create standards that are more realistic, and managers who are more committed to meeting the standards.

13

ROI AND DECENTRALIZED MANAGEMENT

*T*op managers are often eager to designate segments of their company as investment centers and use ROI for performance evaluation and control. However, before these managers designate an operation as an investment center, they should be sure it has four important characteristics.

1. Autonomous operations.
2. Free access to vendors and customers.
3. Separate revenues and costs.
4. Management design.

Autonomous Operations

Before top managers can gain the benefits of an investment center, they must be certain the segment is an independent operating unit. The segment manager must control most operating decisions, subject only to broad policy guidance from top management. Investment in capital assets, asset maintenance schedules, production volumes, product mix, and prices must all be controlled completely or in large measure by the segment manager.

Examples of segments where this level of independent operating control is possible include manufacturing operations, retail and wholesale outlets, and customer service and repair centers. Segments such as advertising departments, internal maintenance departments, and personnel usually cannot be independent in the same way and cannot be investment centers evaluated by ROI.

Although complete decentralization is not a prerequisite for independent segments, autonomous operating units are common to decentralized companies. The intuitive image of a decentralized company is one with geographically dispersed branches (see Exhibit 13–1), but decentralized management does not require physically separate operating segments. Decentralized management delegates decision-making authority to lower-level operating managers, as shown in Exhibit 13–2. These managers are often more responsive than headquarters staff to the conditions in their operating units.

In contrast, centralized management retains direct control of operations, and lower-level managers do not make major decisions. The advantages and disadvantages of decentralized and centralized management are listed in Exhibits 13–3 and 13–4.

EXHIBIT 13–1
Geographic Decentralization with Production in Each Location

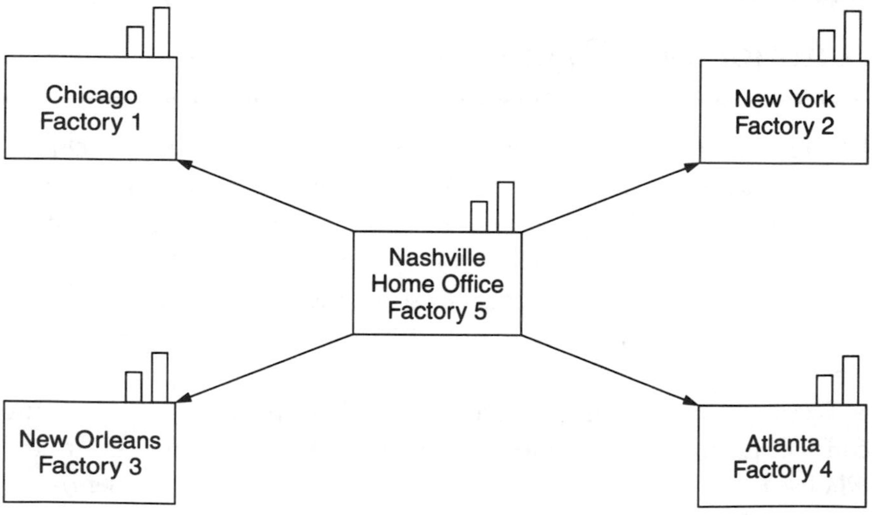

EXHIBIT 13–2
Decentralized Management with Authority in Each Department

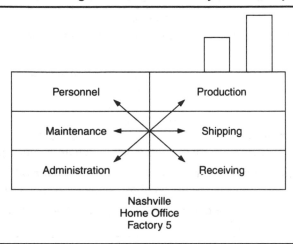

Personnel Production

Maintenance Shipping

Administration Receiving

Nashville
Home Office
Factory 5

EXHIBIT 13–3
The Advantages and Disadvantages of Decentralized Management

Advantages

Quicker Decisions. Because details are not required to travel up and down the management pyramid, decisions are made more quickly.

More Responsive Decisions. Decisions made by operating managers are often more responsive to current conditions.

More Specialization. Operating managers focus on operations, and top management focuses on strategic planning.

Improved Motivation. Managers who participate in decisions are better motivated than those who enforce directives from headquarters.

Disadvantages

Suboptimization. Individual segment managers may maximize their own separate profits rather than working for the good of the company as a whole.

Performance Evaluation. It is difficult to evaluate the performances of individual operating managers whose activities are different.

EXHIBIT 13–4
The Advantages and Disadvantages of Centralized Management

Advantages

Better Control. Centralized management can easily focus on a clear corporate goal.

Economies of Scale. One large operation is often more efficient than several smaller, decentralized operations.

Disadvantages

Increased Complexity. Large, centrally controlled entities that combine several different operations are often complex and hard to manage effectively.

Diseconomies of Scale. Large operations are often more difficult to control and keep efficient than are several smaller, decentralized operations.

Span of Control. The larger an operation grows, the more difficult it is to control everything from the top.

Free Access to Vendors and Customers

An investment center manager must have free access to suppliers and markets, both inside and outside the company. The manager must be able to barter for the lowest cost when buying, and to demand the best price when selling. For example, the manager of a segment that uses copper wire must be free to buy from the company's copper wire production segment, or, if price, quality, or service is better, from outside the company. The same conditions must apply to the copper production segment (if it is to be an investment center): it must be able to sell its wire outside the company if a better price is offered.

If segment managers are not free to improve their return because top management restricts sales or purchases to particular units within the company, the managers' morale and incentive will be reduced. With free access to suppliers and markets, each autonomous segment will find the most efficient, effective, economical methods for purchasing, production, and marketing.

Segments that cannot compete with markets or suppliers outside the company will not survive. If the copper wire operation cannot successfully produce copper wire and sell it to the downstream segment in competition with outside producers, the company as a whole is better off discontinuing the operation.

Separate Revenues and Costs

An investment center must be able to separate its costs and revenues from those of the rest of the company. Without this ability, the segment cannot determine a profit "return." If a segment "sells" its production to another segment in the same company, there may be a degree of arbitrariness regarding the selling or transfer price established between the two operations. If the production is specialized—perhaps tailor-made for use in the downstream division's operation—there may be no realistic way to set an objective price. (The problem of objective price is discussed in Chapter 14.)

Management Design

Management must consider the objectives of a segment and decide whether the segment will be most focused on its objectives if it operates as an investment center. For example, assume a molding operation receives its molding compounds from an upstream department, molds the compounds into reinforced components, and then "sells" (transfers) the components to a downstream department for use in a finished product. There are alternative sources for the molding compounds, and alternative customers to whom the molding operation could sell its production. Thus, the molding operation could operate as an investment center.

EXHIBIT 13–5
Management Design May Change the Goals of a Department

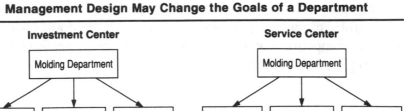

But suppose top management wants the molding operation to perform a research and development function by (1) conducting test runs using experimental molding compounds, and (2) molding experimental component designs for the downstream department. The managers of the segments could negotiate in the market (outside the company) for the research and development services performed by the molding department, but trade secrets might be stolen and, even if a premium were paid, experimental work might not be given a high priority.

In such circumstances, management may not intend for the molding operation to place a high priority on profit; instead, it would gain its value, in part, from its research and development role (see Exhibit 13–5). Thus, the molding department is best managed as a service center, not an investment center.

Some segments may completely lose their usefulness by operating as investment centers. The company may, for instance, employ in its market research department high-powered experts who are capable of operating as an autonomous consulting group, offering services to clients inside and outside of the company. However, to undertake market research in this way defeats the purpose of the department. The operating objective of the market research group must be to improve the market position of the company, not to create a segment profit. The legal department, public relations department, and other service departments would also be bad choices for investment centers.

14

ROI AND TRANSFERS BETWEEN SEGMENTS

*I*nvestment centers' need for separable revenues and costs is not a problem when there are alternative vendors and customers outside the company. With these sources available, segments can buy, sell, and transfer products from one to the other at competitive market prices. Company investment can then be directed to activities that generate the best returns. Conversely, if a segment grows inefficient and cannot operate in competition with producers outside the company, it will find no customers for its output inside or outside the company, and will be unable to continue. Investment in unprofitable operations is moved to profitable operations. If a segment competes successfully with suppliers outside the company, it will find customers for its output, and its profitability will justify requests for additional capital or other support.

Problems occur when there is no alternative vendor or customer, and no true market reference price. In this situation, managers often create pseudomarket transfer prices based on several different general models. Attempts to contrive an artificial measure to replace market price have the potential to cause problems and reduce ROI.

The most common problems associated with pseudomarket transfer prices include:

1. Capital investments are misdirected, based on contrived, artificial returns.

2. Operating funds are misdirected because budgets are based on contrived cost and revenue figures.

3. Bonuses and other performance rewards are based on assessments that use negotiated or mandated results rather than real costs and revenues.

4. Erroneous actions are taken because evaluations of problems and opportunities are distorted by ignorance of true revenues and costs (including opportunity costs).

5. Responses to changes in markets and competitors are inappropriate due to contrived costs and revenues.

6. Morale is poor among segment managers because of their perceptions of different treatment among segments.

Transfer Prices

Transfer prices, used in place of actual market prices established in competition with producers outside the company, vary greatly in their usefulness and their potential for harm. The following methods of setting transfer prices are widely used.

Published Market Prices

Many companies that do not allow segments to buy or sell outside the company use published market prices to transfer intermediate products between segments. Published market prices are also adapted for use as transfer prices when the actual intermediate product is of a different type, grade, or quality than a product whose prices are published.

Often, published prices of intermediate products are for different quantities of product, in a different location, than the product transferred. Published prices are usually spot prices rather than long-term contract prices, which are more suitable to the relationship between a company's segments. Adjustments are made for these differences:

Published spot price	$107
Quality upgrade	12
Quantity discount	(9)
Shipping cost adjustment	5
Sales commission saving	(20)
Required packaging	22
Transfer price	$117

Using published market prices either directly or adjusted for differences is strongly recommended. Such prices realistically approximate the prices that would be obtained in a competitive transfer pricing system.

Marginal Cost

Marginal cost is the additional cost required for a segment to produce an additional unit of product or service. Most frequently, this cost is for raw material and labor, plus whatever components of overhead costs (such as electricity or lubricant) are increased when additional units are produced.

Materials used:		
Lumber	$23	
Fasteners	2	
L-brackets	12	$ 37
Labor used:		
Assembly hours 2 × $18		36
Marginal overhead		41
Transfer price		$114

Most overhead costs are related to the capacity to produce and do not increase when additional units are produced. Property taxes, lease

EXHIBIT 14–1
Transfer Prices and Profit

Type of Transfer Price	Amount of Transfer Price	Total Cost per Unit	Profit (Loss) per Unit
Marginal cost	$114.00	$168.00	($58.00)
Full cost	168.00	168.00	-0-
Marginal cost plus markup (65%)	188.10*	168.00	20.10
Full cost plus markup (30%)	218.40**	168.00	50.40

* $114 × 1.65 = $188.10.
** $168 × 1.30 = $218.40.

payments, and supervisory salaries are common overhead costs that are not increased when additional units are produced.

Marginal costs are useless in calculating the profit generated by the segment producing the transferred product because the total cost of production will always include capacity costs above the marginal cost of production (as illustrated in Exhibit 14–1). Marginal cost provides information useful for short-term operating decisions, such as pricing for special orders or promotions. A special order or promotion should not be priced below the total marginal cost of production in all segments unless the company is willing to sustain a loss.

Perhaps the biggest disadvantage of marginal cost as a transfer price is that production inefficiencies are hidden and are passed along to downstream segments. The inefficiencies of one segment are masked by the efficiencies of the next.

Full Cost

Full cost, the total amount required for a segment to produce a product or service, consists of raw material, labor, and an allocated portion of all overhead costs (including capacity costs that do not increase when additional units are produced).

Materials used:		
Lumber	$23	
Fasteners	2	
L-brackets	12	$ 37
Labor used:		
Assembly hours 2 × $18		36
Full overhead per unit		95
Transfer price		$168

Full costs are useless in calculating the profit generated by the segment producing the transferred product because the total cost of production will be approximately equal to the transfer "revenue" (see Exhibit 14–1). Unlike marginal cost, full cost does not provide information useful for short-term operating decisions, but it is important in pricing production in the normal course of business. A product must be priced above its total full cost of production in all segments if the company is to earn a profit.

The biggest disadvantage of full cost is that, like marginal cost, it has the potential for inefficiencies to be hidden and passed along to downstream segments.

Markups on Cost

To make cost-based transfer prices appear more useful, many companies add an arbitrary profit markup. The markup can be applied to marginal or full cost, as illustrated in Exhibit 14–1. Using a markup on cost allows a segment manager to prepare an income statement, show a profit, and report an ROI. Cost-plus transfer prices then appear to perform like true market price transfer prices, but they do not.

Cost-plus transfer prices do not bring the discipline of competition to producing segments. They are authoritarian and arbitrary. Most commonly, they are set by top management using a markup return based on the company's ultimate gross profit on sales when it sells to customers outside the company, or some measure of the company's or the segment's cost of capital. Another approach to setting a segment markup is to allow a segment manager to earn the profit he or she feels would be necessary when selling to an outside customer. Neither approach creates a competitive market price.

15

WEIGHTED AVERAGE
COST OF CAPITAL

The minimum rate of return is the rate of return that a company forgoes by investing in one particular project rather than investing in an alternative project of comparable risk. This rate should be equal to the company's cost of capital. The cost of capital is the weighted average of the costs of debt and equity financing used to generate capital for investments; it is the rate that results from obtaining funds from both stockholders and creditors. The cost of debt results from paying interest to creditors. The cost of equity is the return required by stockholders for the risk of supplying capital to the company. The weighted average cost of capital (WACC) is the weighted average cost of these funds and represents the minimum acceptable rate that an investment project must earn if the company is to pay interest to its creditors and provide its stockholders with their desired rate of return.

Calculating the WACC

To compute the cost of creditor capital, many companies start with the effective rate of interest on debt. If a company pays $20,000 a year in interest on a note with a principal amount of $200,000, then the effective rate of interest is 10 percent ($20,000/$200,000). Because interest on debt is tax-deductible, this rate is adjusted for the income tax saved. Assuming a tax rate of 35 percent, each additional dollar of interest costs the company only $0.65 because taxes are reduced by $0.35 for each additional interest dollar. However, this approach is simplistic because companies issue many different types of debt instruments (e.g., zero coupon bonds, convertible bonds, commodity-backed bonds, pay-in-kind debentures, and floating-rate notes). Finding the effective rate of interest can be very complicated.

Calculating the rate associated with stockholders' equity is even more complicated because it relates to stockholders' expectations regarding a combination of future earnings, share appreciation, and dividend payments. One way to calculate the cost of equity capital is to divide expected earnings per share by the market price of the company's stock. If the company expects per-share earnings of $1.50 and the market price of its stock is $10.00 per share, the cost of equity capital is 15 percent. Complications in the calculation arise because, similar to debt instruments, there are many different types of equity items (e.g., different classes of common stock, adjusted-rate preferred stock, and redeemable preferred stock). Each type of instrument has its own distinctive features. Additionally, expectations regarding future growth may be significantly different from the current return evidenced by the dividend per share divided by the current market price.

We can calculate a WACC using the data from above and a company's capital structure of 60 percent debt and 40 percent equity. With an income tax rate of 35 percent, the calculation results in a WACC of 9.9 percent.

Weighted cost of debt + Weighted cost of equity = WACC
(0.10 interest on debt × [1 − 0.35] 0.60) + (0.15 cost of equity × 0.40)
= 0.099 = 9.9%

Again, this approach is very simplistic. However, the analysis provided should give you an idea of how a company calculates its cost of capital. Because of the numerous types of debt and equity instruments, there is no general agreement on calculating the WACC, and the calculation poses a challenge even for the most sophisticated company manager. There is a general agreement, however, that the WACC is a good indicator of the riskiness of a company: the higher the risk, the higher the WACC.

Calculating cost of capital assumes that the company will continue to raise capital in the proportions used in the calculation. However, strict proportions are difficult to maintain. Expected future changes in the proportions of capital should be factored into the analysis of the WACC.

Other Estimates of WACC

Because of the complexities associated with different types of financial instruments, many managers take a judgmental approach to determining WACC: they use the rate of interest paid on U.S. Treasury bonds, bills, or notes. This rate is adjusted upward for the riskiness of the company, based on the manager's assessment of the company, its industry, and the overall market. The resultant rate is normally referred to as the real rate of interest.

Or, a manager might experiment with various rates, using a trial-and-error approach. A manager might feel that the resulting benefits of improved accuracy of the estimate are not justified because of the cost associated with the complicated calculations and the subjectivity of the assumptions.

A company might also use the rate of return on its capital or financial assets as a surrogate for WACC. In computing this ratio, the numerator is a measure of cash return rather than an amount such as net income, which includes accrued amounts that may not reflect net cash inflows.

Another alternative a company can use is the nominal rate of interest. The nominal rate is defined as the real rate of interest plus an adjustment for inflation, making the nominal rate higher than the real rate of interest.

Finally, a manager must decide whether the cost of capital should be computed on a before- or after-tax basis. This consideration is important because, with income tax rates rising to nearly 40 percent, there is a substantial difference in the cost-of-capital computation.

Additional Factors Relating to WACC

One company-wide WACC is not normally used. We calculate one overall rate to simplify our discussion; however, different operating segments are likely to have different degrees of risk. Thus, more than one method is used to calculate WACC in determining how much return a company should earn. Finally, the use of an inappropriate rate could lead managers to accept or reject projects erroneously and may result in a lower ROI.

16

THE TIME VALUE OF MONEY

When state lotteries make million-dollar payoffs, they normally pay these amounts over payout periods of 10, 20, or 30 years. Publishers' Clearinghouse and The Reader's Digest mail sweepstakes are other examples of substantial money prizes being paid to winners over some future period of time. In some instances, though, winners have the option of accepting a lump-sum payment rather than receiving payments over a stipulated period. Would you prefer $2.4 million today or $120,000 per year for 20 years (a total of $2.4 million)? All things equal, and ignoring income tax considerations, you should opt for the $2.4 million today because a dollar received today is worth more than a dollar to be received at some time in the future. Money received today is worth more because it can be invested, and today's dollars will yield more than the invested amount over a period of years. If the amount to be received is $2.4 million today versus $130,000 per year for 20 years (a total of $2.6 million), the analysis becomes more complicated; however, the basic premise is still the same: the *time value of money* is important in any situation where you will receive or pay cash at some future point or points in time.

The Concept of Present Value

The time value of money is an important consideration in many capital budgeting decisions (e.g., acquiring machinery or building a new plant). Discounted cash flow techniques (discussed in Chapter 18), such as net present value, present value index, and internal rate of return, consider the time value of money in making capital budgeting decisions. These project valuation techniques consider the time value of money by comparing the cash outflow at the beginning of a proposed project with the anticipated cash inflows to be generated by the project. A valid comparison cannot be made using absolute dollar amounts of the inflows or outflow because money has a time value. As we previously stated, the right to receive $100 today is worth more than the right to receive $100 in, say, two years, because that $100 can be invested to earn interest over the two-year period. Discounting, or calculating present values, is used to evaluate future cash inflows relating to investment decisions.

Discounted cash flow refers to the present value, at a point in time, of a stream of receipts or payments to be received or paid in the future. The receipts or payments pattern is called an annuity. The concept of present value is related to the application of compound interest. Earning interest on interest as well as on principal is referred to as *compounding*. For example, assume that we invest $1,000 in a savings account at a rate of 10 percent compounded annually. The balance in the account after five years would be $1,611, computed as follows:

Year	(a) Principal at Beginning of Year	(b) Interest at 10%	(a + b) Principal at End of Year
1	$1,000	$1,000 × 10% = $100	$1,100
2	1,100	1,100 × 10% = 110	1,210
3	1,210	1,210 × 10% = 121	1,331
4	1,331	1,331 × 10% = 133	1,464
5	1,464	1,464 × 10% = 147	1,611

At a 10 percent interest rate, the future value of $1,000 deposited today would grow to $1,611 at the end of five years. This sequence of deposits is depicted in the following time line.

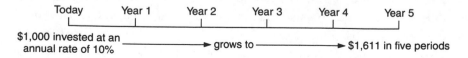

Today　　　Year 1　　　Year 2　　　Year 3　　　Year 4　　　Year 5

$1,000 invested at an annual rate of 10% ———→ grows to ———→ $1,611 in five periods

There are formulas for calculating future and present values. Let us assume that

F_n = the future value of an amount at the end of the stipulated time period
i = the annual rate of interest
n = number of periods
P = the principal amount

The formula for the future value of an investment is

$$F_n = P(1 + i)^n$$

Using the amount and interest rate in our example, $F_n = \$1,000$ $(1 + 0.10)^5 = 1.611$. We can express

$$F_n = P(1 + i)^n$$

as

$$F_n = P \times [\text{Table}(i,n)]$$

where Table (i,n) is the future value interest factor for $1, found in the table derived from this formula. The future value of $1 invested today, calculated for various interest rates and time periods, is shown in Table 16–1. You can see that the value for five periods at 10 percent interest rate is 1.611.

The present value of an amount views the compound interest concept in reverse; that is, the present value of the $1,611 to be received five periods from now is $1,000:

| Today | Year 1 | Year 2 | Year 3 | Year 4 | Year 5 |

$1,000 invested at an annual rate of 10% ◄─── grows to ◄─── $1,611 in five periods

Present value factors are computed in the same manner, using the present value formula, which we will not present here. An example of a present value table for five periods, at various interest rates, is presented in Table 16–2. (Many calculators and computer programs include future and present value functions.)

TABLE 16–1
Future Value of $1 Due in N Periods

No. of Periods	Interest Rate							
	1%	4%	5%	6%	8%	10%	12%	15%
1	1.010	1.040	1.050	1.060	1.080	1.100	1.120	1.150
2	1.020	1.082	1.103	1.124	1.166	1.210	1.254	1.323
3	1.030	1.125	1.158	1.191	1.260	1.331	1.405	1.521
4	1.041	1.170	1.216	1.263	1.361	1.464	1.574	1.749
5	1.051	1.217	1.276	1.338	1.469	1.611	1.762	2.011

From Table 16–2, we can see that the present value factor of $1 for five periods at 10 percent is 0.621. Multiplying $1,611 by 0.621 results in a present value of $1,000 (rounded).

The present value of an annuity is simply the combined present values of the individual payments or receipts discounted back to today. Suppose we wish to know whether we should accept a lump sum of $3,500 today, or five receipts of $1,000 each, to be received at the end of each of the periods. The interest rate is 8 percent. Using the present

TABLE 16–2
Present Value of $1 Due in N Periods

No. of Periods	Interest Rate							
	1%	4%	5%	6%	8%	10%	12%	15%
1	0.990	0.962	0.952	0.943	0.926	0.909	0.893	0.870
2	0.980	0.925	0.907	0.890	0.857	0.826	0.797	0.756
3	0.971	0.890	0.864	0.840	0.794	0.751	0.712	0.658
4	0.961	0.855	0.823	0.792	0.735	0.683	0.636	0.572
5	0.951	0.822	0.784	0.747	0.681	0.621	0.567	0.497

value factors from Table 16–2, we can calculate the present value of this annuity to be:

	Number of Periods				
	1	2	3	4	5

Present
Value

$\ \ \ 926 = \longleftarrow$ $1,000 × 0.926

$\ \ \ \ \ 857 = \longleftarrow$ $1,000 × 0.857

$\ \ \ \ \ 794 = \longleftarrow$ $1,000 × 0.794

$\ \ \ \ \ 735 = \longleftarrow$ $1,000 × 0.735

$\ \ \ \ \ \underline{681} = \longleftarrow$ $1,000 × 0.681

$\underline{\underline{\$3,993}}$

Because the present value of the receipts is greater than the lump sum, receiving the annuity would be better than the lump sum (all other factors considered equal, and ignoring income taxes).

Formulas for calculating the present value of annuities (now shown here) can be used to derive factors for an annuity table. Table 16–3 is an example of an annuity table.

Keep in mind that the present value of an annuity is the combined present values of the individual payments or receipts discounted back to today. In Table 16–2, if we add the individual present value factors for five periods at 8 percent, we obtain 3.993 (0.926 + 0.857 +

TABLE 16–3
Present Value of $1 to Be Received Periodically for N Periods

No. of Periods	Interest Rate								
	1%	4%	5%	6%	8%	10%	12%	14%	15%
1	0.990	0.962	0.952	0.943	0.926	0.909	0.893	0.877	0.870
2	1.970	1.886	1.859	1.833	1.783	1.736	1.690	1.647	1.626
3	2.941	2.775	2.723	2.673	2.577	2.487	2.402	2.322	2.283
4	3.902	3.630	3.546	3.465	3.312	3.170	3.037	2.914	2.855
5	4.853	4.452	4.329	4.212	3.993	3.791	3.605	3.433	3.352

0.794 + 0.735 + 0.681), which is the present value factor for the annuity at 8 percent, for five periods, as shown in Table 16–3.

Example 1

The company controller wants to know what amount will be on deposit in four years if he invests $4,300 at 12 percent today. The amount is:

Present value × Table 16–1 value = Future value

$4,300   ×   1.574   = $6,768

If $4,300 is invested today at 12 percent annual interest, it will be worth $6,768 in four years.

Example 2

Your son will be attending college in four years. You want to have the total amount of his tuition on hand when be begins his studies. The anticipated cost of tuition in four years is $25,000. If the interest rate is 8 percent, what amount would you need to deposit today in order to have $25,000 on hand in four years? The present value of $25,000 due in four years at 8 percent is:

Future value × Table 16–2 value = Present value

$25,000   ×   0.735   = $18,375

You would have to invest $18,375 today, at 8 percent, to have $25,000 in the tuition account in four years.

Example 3

A friend has won a lottery. She was given the option of taking a $4,000 lump-sum payment today or receiving a $1,000 payment for each of the next five years. At an interest rate of 12 percent, the present value of an annuity of $1,000 for five periods is:

$$\text{Periodic payment} \times \text{Table 16–3 value} = \text{Present value}$$
$$\$1,000 \quad \times \quad 3.605 \quad = \quad \$3,605$$

All things being equal, your friend should take the lump-sum payment.

Example 4

You are examining whether your company should buy (by obtaining a mortgage) or lease a warehouse. The lessor has quoted an annual lease payment of \$120,000 for each of the next 5 years. The warehouse has a fair market value of \$400,000 today, the annual interest rate is 10 percent, and the mortgage note would be paid off in five equal installments over the next 5 years. You need to know the mortgage payment amount for 5 years at 10 percent and compare it to the annual lease payments.

$$\text{Periodic payment} \times \text{Table 16–3 value} = \text{Present value}$$
$$\text{Periodic payment} \times \quad 3.791 \quad = \$400,000$$
$$\text{Periodic payment} \qquad\qquad = \frac{\$400,000}{3.791} = \$105,513$$

Again, all things equal, your company should buy rather than lease the warehouse.

17

CAPITAL BUDGETING

*I*ndividuals invest in long-lived assets such as their homes, major appliances, automobiles, and furniture. Companies also make investment decisions that impact operations for several periods. Investments in long-lived assets are referred to in financial statements as capital assets. The decisions that evolve from analysis of their purchase are called capital budgeting decisions.

Stockholders expect companies to protect their equity. Because a company has limited resources, management must use capital investments as effectively as possible. Therefore, a company's capital expenditure program needs to make capital allocations in order of priority and within stipulated boundaries of allocated funds if it is to generate profits and increase returns to its stockholders.

Capital budgeting decisions generally fall into one of two classifications: acquisition decisions and replacement decisions.

- Acquisition decisions relate to the selection of new facilities or the expansion of existing facilities. Examples include investments in long-lived assets such as property, plant, equipment, and resource commitments for product development and market research.

- Replacement decisions relate to replacing existing facilities with new facilities. Examples include replacement of a manual accounting system with a computerized system, or replacing an inefficient refrigeration system with a new up-to-date system.

Acquisition and replacement decisions are discussed in an excerpt from the 1994 annual report of Ball Corporation (Exhibit 17–1). Ball Corporation produces metal and glass packaging products primarily

EXHIBIT 17–1
Ball Corporation Management's Discussion and Analysis
December 31, 1994

The company has signed a definitive agreement with Datum Inc. for the sale of the Efratom unit for approximately $26.5 million to be paid in a combination of cash and Datum common stock. The sale is expected to take place late in the first quarter of 1995. In addition, a new subsidiary, Earth-Watch, Inc., was formed in the aerospace and communications segment in late 1994 to serve the market for satellite-based remote sensing of the earth. During 1994 the company undertook a study to explore various strategic options for the remaining aerospace and communications segment. The study was concluded with a decision to retain the core aerospace and communications business.

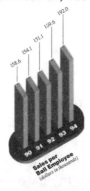

Heekin operating cash flow was offset by reduced operating performance, principally in the glass container and aerospace and communications operations.

Working capital at December 31, 1994, excluding short-term debt and the current portion of long-term debt, was $315.1 million, a decrease of $49.7 million from the 1993 year end, reflecting increased accounts payable and accrued liabilities. The current ratio was 1.40 and 1.53 at December 31, 1994 and 1993, respectively.

Capital expenditures of $94.5 million in 1994 were primarily for conversions of metal beverage plant equipment to new industry container specifications, expansion of warehouse space for metal beverage containers, furnace rebuilds and capacity optimization at certain glass container plants, and productivity improvement programs in several of the metal food container plants. Property, plant and equipment expenditures amounted to $140.9 million in 1993 and were primarily for conversions of metal beverage plant equipment to new industry specifications, expansion of the Fairfield, California, plant to accommodate additional business, completion of the Ruston, Louisiana, glass container plant

Financial Position, Liquidity and Capital Resources

Cash flow from operations of $240.7 million in 1994 increased from $120.2 million in 1993. The 1993 amount excludes the effects of the sale of $66.5 million of trade accounts receivable. The increased cash flow from operations in 1994 reflects higher annual operating earnings and significantly improved fourth quarter performance. Operating cash flow in 1993, excluding the effect of the receivable sale, was essentially unchanged from 1992, as the additional

PEOPLE

When there's an important decision to be made at Ball Corporation's Williamsburg, Virginia, or Burlington, Ontario, plant, employee teams will be a part of the process.

The same is true at other plants as well, as employees tackle production questions and a host of other issues.

Williamsburg's 13-member steering commit-tee, one of the oldest and strongest at any Ball plant, meets regularly to solve problems that might interfere with the goal: to make top quality cans efficiently.

Employees from every area of the plant – such as (left to right) Calvin Boone, maintainer; Bob Martin, engineering manager; Marjorie Daniel, human resource manager; Larry Otey, maintainer; and Tommy Nguyen, maintainer – make significant contributions as part of the steering committee.

Burlington provides another example of what employee teams can accomplish. The Burlington Recycling Team has reduced the amount of waste leaving the plant by 36 percent, thereby helping the environment and contributing to profit improvement.

(continued)

EXHIBIT 17–1 (continued)

expansion and the Quebec food container manufacturing consolidation, and a number of furnace rebuilds in glass container plants. Property, plant and equipment expenditures amounted to $110.2 million in 1992 and included completion of a fourth aluminum beverage can line in Saratoga Springs, New York, consolidation of Quebec food container operations, and expansion of the Ruston, Louisiana, glass manufacturing facility, as well as normal expenditures for upgrades of glass forming equipment and furnace rebuilds.

In 1995 total capital spending of approximately $280.0 million is anticipated. This includes significant amounts for emerging business opportunities, such as domestic plastics (PET) and metal packaging in China, and spending in existing businesses, in part to complete the conversion of metal beverage equipment to the new industry specifications.

Premiums on company owned life insurance were approximately $20.0 million each year. Amounts in the Consolidated Statement of Cash Flows represent net cash flows from this program including related tax benefits. The company borrowed $23.4 million and $37.2 million in 1994 and 1993, respectively, from the accumulated net cash value.

At December 31, 1994, indebtedness decreased by $143.5 million from the year earlier to $493.7 million. The reduction in debt was achieved as a result of positive cash flow from operations. The consolidated debt-to-total capitalization ratio at December 31, 1994, improved to 43.8 percent compared with 52.6 percent at December 31, 1993. The improved ratio was primarily the result of higher earnings, reduced common dividends and the reduction in debt. The company has revolving facilities of $300.0 million consisting of a $150.0 million, three-year facility and 364-day facilities which amount to $150.0 million.

During 1993 the company took advantage of low prevailing interest rates by prepaying

Top seven states and provinces in number of Ball employees:
Colorado – 2,202
California – 1,361
Illinois – 1,246
Ohio – 1,125
Indiana – 1,029
Pennsylvania – 777
Ontario – 709

Ball is a founding member of the National Association of Manufacturers, which is celebrating its centennial. Manufacturing employs approximately 18 million people in the U.S. On average, manufacturing jobs pay 15 percent more than jobs elsewhere in the economy.

$20.0 million of serial notes, and by refinancing $108.8 million of Heekin indebtedness and $17.0 million of industrial development revenue bonds. The company redeemed the Series C Preferred Stock on January 7, 1992, for $50.3 million. In the last half of 1992, the company borrowed approximately $214.0 million of fixed-rate, long-term debt, the proceeds of which were used to repay floating-rate, short-term debt. Short-term debt had increased primarily due to financing the acquisition of the Kerr assets, the redemption of the Series C Preferred Stock, and the increase in working capital.

Cash dividends paid on common stock in 1994 were $0.60 per share. The reduction in the common dividend in 1994 from $1.24 paid in 1993 provided improved financial flexibility and access to capital. Management believes that, absent a major business dislocation, existing credit resources will be adequate to meet foreseeable financing requirements of the company's businesses.

Restructuring and Other Charges

In the company's major packaging markets, excess manufacturing capacity and severe pricing pressures presented significant competitive challenges in recent years. Although domestic metal beverage container operations have operated at or near capacity, such has not been the case in the metal food and glass container businesses, including the Heekin business acquired in 1993. More recently, reductions in federal defense expenditures and other attempts to curb the federal budget deficit have created similar market dynamics in the aerospace and defense industry as the number of new contract bidding opportunities has declined and existing programs have been curtailed or delayed.

In late 1993 the company developed plans to restructure the company's businesses in order to adapt the company's manufacturing capabilities and administrative organizations for foods and beverages, and provides aerospace and communications products and services to government and commercial customers.

Perhaps the most critical aspect of the capital budgeting process is estimating the cash flows that are associated with alternative projects. A company must estimate not only how much cash is to be paid or received but also when the cash will be paid or received. This task is made more difficult because the cash flows that will occur depend on the following:

1. The economic environment of the company and its industry.
2. The strategic plans of the company.
3. World events and trends.
4. Other natural and unnatural events beyond the control of the company.

To deal with this aspect of the process, management brings together a capital budgeting team that is competent in all of these areas. Assumptions are made by the team as to the expected cash flows. Sensitivity analysis is used to assess the validity of those assumptions. (Sensitivity analysis refers to the determination of how sensitive the calculation is to errors in predicting one or more input values. It involves trying to find out how much a factor would increase or decrease before a different decision would be indicated.) This is a necessary part of the process because the company's projection of cash flows is only as reliable as the quality of the assumptions that support that forecast of cash flows.

Cash Flow Forecast and Project Life

The capital budgeting cash flow forecast provides an estimate of cash flows for the lives of each of the alternative projects. These forecasts are used as the basis for capital budgeting computations. Management needs to know the exact timing of cash inflows and outflows because, at these points, the composition of the company's assets changes and its financial position is altered. At each of these points, management has committed funds that are no longer available for other investment opportunities. The capital outlay can only be recovered through the benefits received from the outlay (e.g., knowledge from market research) or the use of the capital asset (e.g., as in the case of the purchase of a new plant asset). Because capital budgeting mistakes can be very costly, careful attention must be paid to every detail.

Defining the project and predicting its outcome are the most challenging and difficult parts of the capital budgeting process. The time horizon, which may span many years, makes it difficult to assess what lies ahead. For example, in the early years of a project, many costs are easy to estimate; in later years, the nature of the costs may be virtually unknown. Likewise, the perceived benefits of a project may not be realized for years. Translating costs and benefits into cash flows is difficult because many costs and benefits are not easy to quantify. Failure to include an item implicitly assigns a cash flow of zero to that item. Such an omission can have a significant impact on whether an investment proposal is accepted or rejected.

Finally, looking into the future requires management to use imperfect information, which limits the predictive accuracy. Just because a computer program provides a quantitative solution down to the thousandth of a penny does not mean it's precise; remember that capital budgeting decisions are made using estimates.

The Effect of the Depreciation Tax Shield on Cash Flows

Long-term commitments for capital expenditures and their related cash flows are closely akin to the concept of ROI. Also, tax considerations play a vital role in decisions relating to capital and other major expenditures. Most managers view cash flows on an after-tax basis—that is, after the revenues less expenditures (including any initial outlay) are reduced by the amount of any income taxes due. For example, if an investment project generates taxable revenue, the cash inflows from that project will be reduced by the income taxes paid by the company on that revenue. Similarly, if a project has expenditures that are tax-deductible, cash inflows from the project will be increased by the tax savings resulting from the decrease in income taxes paid. Managers use after-tax cash flows because a project that is appealing on a before-tax basis might later be rejected when examined on an after-tax basis. Revenue and expenses, not cash flows, affect income taxes.

For example, assume that General Motors Corporation (GMC) is contemplating a new promotional campaign in an attempt to boost the sales of its redesigned Chevy truck. The new promotional campaign will cost $200,000. Is this $200,000 the real cost of the promotional campaign to GMC? Assuming sales of $1,500,000 per year, operating expenses of $765,000, and an income tax rate of 40 percent, the following comparison is made by GMC's management:

	No New Promotional Campaign	New Promotional Campaign
Sales	$1,500,000	$1,500,000
Less: Operating expenses	765,000	765,000
Promotional campaign	0	200,000
Income before income taxes	735,000	535,000
Income taxes at 40%	294,000	214,000
Net income	$ 441,000	$ 321,000

The difference in the net incomes is $120,000 ($441,000 without the new campaign minus $321,000 with the new campaign); that is, net income is $120,000 lower if GMC elects to initiate the new promotional campaign. This analysis tells GMC's management that the real cost of the $200,000 promotional expenditure is $120,000 on an after-tax basis. The formula used to determine the after-tax cost of an expenditure can be stated as:

$$\text{Expenditure} \times (1 - \text{Tax rate}) = \text{After-tax cost (cash flow)}$$

Using the data from our example, we see that

$$\$200,000 \times (1 - 40\%) = \$120,000$$

This formula can be applied to any situation, whether the cash flow is an outflow (as it is above) or an inflow. The $200,000 expenditure is considered a "tax shield" because it protects from taxation $200,000 in revenues. In effect, the depreciation tax shield reduces GMC's taxes by $80,000 ($294,000 − $214,000), permitting the company to use these funds for other purposes. (Income taxes differ by $80,000: $294,000 with no new campaign, and $214,000 with the new campaign.) Applying the formula assumes that the outflow is deductible and the inflow is taxable.

Effect of Depreciation on Income Taxes and Cash Flows

Depreciation expense is the charging off of a cost previously incurred and is not accompanied by outflows of cash. However, because depreciation lowers income, it has an indirect effect on cash flow: it reduces the amount of income taxes a company pays, and a reduction of income taxes paid results in an increased cash flow.[1]

To illustrate, assume that Wilson Company is considering producing and selling a new product. Producing the new product requires the purchase of equipment costing $200,000. The equipment will be

---

[1] The tax code allows corporations to deduct certain capital items in full, instead of depreciating them over their service lives. These items are called "listed property" and the company is limited to a deduction of $17,500 in any given year. If a company places into service capital assets classified as "listed property" costing $200,000 or more the limitation on the deduction is gradually reduced and becomes zero when purchases of these assets exceed $217,500. Our discussion in this chapter relates to companies that make annual capital asset acquisitions greater than this amount and assumes that these assets will be depreciated over their service lives as permitted by the tax code.

depreciated, for both financial reporting and tax purposes, over a five-year period, resulting in depreciation charges of $40,000 per year. Assume that average sales are expected to be $1,400,000 a year, operating expenses are $450,000, and the income tax rate is 40 percent. Due to the fact that the old equipment is obsolete and fully depreciated, there is no change in revenues or expenses no matter what the decision. If management wants to know the impact of the purchase after the initial outlay, a budgeted income statement would show the following:

	Investment in the Equipment	No Investment in the Equipment
Sales	$1,400,000	$1,400,000
Less: Operating expenses	450,000	450,000
Additional depreciation	40,000	0
Income before income taxes	910,000	950,000
Income taxes at 40%	364,000	380,000
Net income	$ 546,000	$ 570,000

If Wilson Company does not invest in the equipment, its net income will be higher by $24,000 ($570,000 − $546,000). On this basis, the project will be rejected.

Now examine the cash flows under each of the alternatives. Assuming that all sales and expenses are in cash, not investing in the equipment yields a cash flow of $570,000. If the company invests in the new equipment, its cash flow rises to $586,000 ($546,000 + the noncash depreciation of $40,000 that was subtracted as an expense). Cash flow is higher when the equipment is purchased because, although depreciation is an expense, it does not result in a cash outflow. That is, Wilson Company deducts depreciation to arrive at current income before taxes and, thus, reduces the amount of income taxes it must pay; however, depreciation is not a cash flow. When cash flows are calculated, depreciation must be added back to net income to arrive at the company's net annual cash flow.

Exhibit 17–2 reproduces the statements of consolidated cash flows from the 1994 annual report of Sherwin-Williams Company. Note

EXHIBIT 17–2
Statements of Consolidated Cash Flows
(in Thousands of Dollars) for the Sherwin-Williams Company

	1994	1993	1992
Operations			
Net income	$186,571	$165,227	$ 62,865
Non-cash adjustments:			
Cumulative effect of changes in accounting methods			81,771
Depreciation	60,571	55,063	51,308
Deferred income tax expense	(18,329)	(21,873)	(5,202)
Provisions for disposition of operations	15,412	7,621	7,735
Provisions for environmental remediation	4,700	4,354	9,450
Amortization of intangible assets	13,153	13,753	14,960
Defined benefit pension plans net credit	(11,379)	(16,113)	(15,896)
Net postretirement benefit plans expense	5,139	2,921	8,834
Other	11,222	16,261	7,491
Change in current items—net:			
Increase in accounts receivable	(11,606)	(19,500)	(30,185)
Decrease (increase) in inventories	(28,748)	(19,553)	15,405
Increase in accounts payable	3,933	23,458	27,981
Increase (decrease) in accrued taxes	964	16,697	(7,968)
Increase in accrued employee welfare costs	5,507	14,957	7,816
Other current items	22,882	13,946	(8,903)
Costs incurred for dispositions of operations	(6,949)	(5,767)	(10,366)
Other	(2,520)	4,528	(2,968)
Net operating cash	250,523	255,980	214,128

(continued)

177

EXHIBIT 17–2 (continued)

	1994	1993	1992
Investing			
Capital expenditures	(78,660)	(62,985)	(68,814)
Decrease (increase) in short-term investments	39,700	(36,689)	(3,011)
Acquisitions of assets	(9,215)	(3,157)	(2,985)
Other	6,347	(5,213)	(272)
Net investing cash	(41,828)	(108,044)	(75,082)
Financing			
Payments of long-term debt	(19,607)	(33,711)	(44,174)
Payments of cash dividends	(48,363)	(44,373)	(38,759)
Proceeds from stock options exercised	6,301	9,535	13,101
Purchases of stock for treasury	(128,148)	(16,144)	(4,349)
Other	2,445	2,148	(930)
Net financing cash	(187,372)	(82,545)	(75,111)
Net increase in cash and cash equivalents	21,323	65,391	63,935
Cash and cash equivalents at beginning of year	230,092	164,701	100,766
Cash and cash equivalents at end of year	$251,415	$230,092	$164,701
Taxes paid on income	$132,573	$102,513	$ 89,297
Interest paid on debt	3,314	7,886	7,508

that depreciation is added back to net income in arriving at net operating cash.

Depreciation as a Tax Shield

Because a company can deduct depreciation in computing its taxable income, and thus reduce expenses, depreciation is a tax shield. That is, depreciation deductions act as a shield against tax payments by reducing the amount of income subject to taxation.

In our example, the depreciation deduction of $40,000-shields from income taxes $40,000 of the $1,400,000 of sales. If the investment in the equipment is not made, total expenses will be lower, and income taxes will be higher by $16,000 ($380,000 − $364,000). The depreciation tax shield actually reduces taxes by $16,000, allowing the company to use the cash for other purposes.

The formula for computing the tax savings resulting from the depreciation tax shield is as follows.

$$\begin{matrix} \text{Annual amount} \\ \text{of depreciation} \end{matrix} \times \text{Tax rate} = \begin{matrix} \text{Tax savings resulting from} \\ \text{depreciation tax shield} \end{matrix}$$

In our example, the tax savings are computed as follows.

$$\$40,000 \times 40\% = \$16,000$$

Because the tax savings can be viewed as a cash inflow, it is an important consideration in capital investment decisions that impact ROI.

Impact of the Modified Accelerated Cost Recovery System (MACRS)

For the sake of illustration, our example assumes that depreciation deductions are on a straight-line basis for both financial reporting and tax purposes. Current tax law requires companies to use the Modified Accelerated Cost Recovery System (MACRS) in computing periodic depreciation deductions for tax purposes.[2] Essentially, MACRS groups assets into one of eight different property classifications; an asset is placed into a classification based on its estimated useful life. Within each classification, a certain percentage of the asset's cost can be deducted as depreciation each year.

In general, the purpose of MACRS is to encourage capital investment by allowing, through depreciation tax deductions, a more rapid recovery of capital investment in the early years of an asset's life. Depreciation deductions for tax purposes are therefore not necessarily the same as those for financial reporting purposes. This difference in deductions must be taken into consideration when examining the tax effects of a proposed capital investment alternative.

---

[2] Companies are not precluded from using the straight-line depreciation method over a life at least as long as the MACRS life.

18

DISCOUNTED CASH FLOW METHODS

A capital budgeting project normally has five phases: (1) project identification, (2) information acquisition, (3) project selection, (4) financing, and (5) project implementation and control. An understanding of each phase is important.

1. *Project identification.* The company looks at its capital expenditure alternatives and decides which project or projects might best achieve its overall organizational goals.

2. *Information acquisition.* The available projects are identified and their predicted outcomes are prepared. Management gathers both quantitative and qualitative information. Quantitative factors, such as cash inflows and outflows, are expressed in numerical terms. Qualitative factors, such as improved product quality or delivery time, normally cannot be measured in numerical terms, but they can be very important and should be considered in capital investment decisions.

3. *Project selection.* Predicted outcomes are reviewed by management, and the financial aspects of each project are analyzed in detail. The following quantitative methods are used to analyze capital budgeting projects:

   a. Discounted cash flow methods

      • Net present value

      • Present value index

      • Internal rate of return

b. Payback

c. Accounting rate of return

This chapter discussed the discounted cash flow project selection methods. Chapter 19 discusses the payback and accounting rate of return project selection methods. These methods can be used alone or in combination.

4. *Financing.* Potential sources of financing are identified. Financing can be generated internally or externally. Working capital is an example of internally generated financing. External financing comes from issuing stock or borrowing funds.

5. *Project implementation and control.* Management undertakes the project and monitors project performance. In many cases, performance monitoring includes a postdecision audit in which the predictions made at the time the project was selected are compared with the actual results.

Description of the Methods

To compare alternative projects, discounted cash flow methods recognize project cash inflows and outflows as if they occur at one point in time. The focus is on cash inflows and outflows as opposed to operating revenues and expenses, and these flows are discounted to give recognition to the time value of money. (The time value of money is discussed in Chapter 16.) The examples in this chapter assume that all cash flows are after-tax amounts; that is, the cash flows are what remains after taking income and adjusting for depreciation (where applicable) and income taxes. In adjusting cash flows for the time value of money, we use the compound interest tables in Chapter 16.

There are three main discounted cash flow methods:

1. Net present value (NPV).

2. Present value index (PVI).

3. Internal rate of return (IRR).

Each method is illustrated with a numerical example. Each of these methods is tested in the capital investment process to assess its impact on ROI. In assessing the desirability of alternative investment proposals, a minimum acceptable rate of return is often compared to the expected rate of return on each of the alternative projects. This minimum rate of return is referred to as the required rate of return, hurdle rate, discount rate, cutoff rate, or weighted average cost of capital. The weighted average cost of capital is discussed in Chapter 15.

Net Present Value

Net present value (NPV) is a discounted cash flow technique where all expected cash inflows and outflows are discounted to the present point in time, using a preselected discount rate. The present values of the inflows are added together, and the initial outlay (and any other subsequent outflows) is subtracted. The difference between the inflows and outflows is the net present value. Only projects with positive NPVs are acceptable because the return from these projects exceeds the discount rate. That is, a positive NPV means the present value of the inflows is greater than the present value of the outflows; thus, the project will earn a return greater than the discount rate used to determine the present value. Conversely, a negative NPV indicates that the project will earn a return less than the discount rate used to determine the present values. See Chapter 16 for a complete discussion of the time value of money.

Calculating Net Present Value

Assume that the administrator of a hospital is considering replacing an old X-ray machine with a new state-of-the-art X-ray machine. The new machine will require an initial investment of $480,000 and will result in decreased labor costs (savings) of $130,000 per year for five years (the life of the new machine). We assume the $130,000 of labor savings are after-tax. The company's discount rate is 8 percent. The NPV is calculated using the data in Table 16–2.

Whenever the NPV is greater than or equal to zero, the project is acceptable. If the NPV is zero, the expected rate of return on the investment is equal to the desired rate of return (discount rate) on the project. For example, if the cost of the project from Table 16–2 was $519,090, the present value of the inflows would be equal to the present value of the outflow. In this case, the discount rate would be exactly 8 percent. A positive NPV indicates that the expected rate exceeds the desired rate. A negative NPV means that the expected rate is less than the desired rate of return. NPV calculations do not result in the exact rate of return unless the NPV happens to be exactly equal to zero. The NPV, calculated from Table 16–2, is a positive $39,090.

		Number of Periods			
	1	2	3	4	5

Present Value

$120,380 = ◄— $130,000 × 0.926
 111,410 = ◄————— $130,000 × 0.857
 103,220 = ◄————————— $130,000 × 0.794
  95,550 = ◄————————————— $130,000 × 0.735
  88,530 = ◄————————————————— $130,000 × 0.681

$519,090   Present value of the inflows (savings)
(480,000)   Present value of the outflows (initial outlay)
$ 39,090   Net present value

Because the NPV is positive, we know the expected rate of return is greater than the discount rate of 8 percent. All other things being equal, the project should be accepted.

When multiple projects are being considered, the general rule is to select the project with the largest NPV. However, NPV should not be used to compare independent projects that do not have approximately the same initial investment, because this type of comparison favors projects with higher NPVs without taking into consideration the capital initially invested in the projects. For example, assume that a company could purchase either of two machines. Machine A costs $80,000 and Machine B costs $37,000. The two projects have NPVs of $4,480 and $3,774, respectively. At first glance, it appears that Machine A is the better investment because it has a larger NPV; however, closer analysis indicates that Machine A provides an NPV ROI of only 5.6 percent ($4,480/$80,000) on its investment. On the other hand, Machine B provides a 10.2 percent NPV ROI ($3,774/$37,000) on its investment.

Using Table 16–3 for the NPV calculation, the present value factor for an annuity of 5 periods at 8 percent is 3.933. (Recall from Chapter 16 that this factor is the sum of the present value factors for each of the five future periods at a discount rate of 8 percent—in this instance, .926 + .857 + .794 + .735 + .681 = 3.993 from Table 16–2.)

The annual savings of $130,000 is multiplied by 3.993 to calculate $519,090 as the present value of the cash inflows (savings). This approach cannot be used when the cash flows are not in the form of an annuity (when they are uneven). Instead, each period's cash flows must be individually discounted to the present, using the discount rate for that period.

Other Considerations

Notice that as the discount rate increases, the present values get smaller. At a 12 percent discount rate, the present value of the inflows is $468,650 ($130,000 × 3.605), and the NPV is a negative $11,350. At 12 percent, the return from the project is less than the 8 percent minimum rate of return. In practice, as the discount rate increases, a manager becomes less likely to accept a particular project.

Two other observations are important:

1. To keep our example simple, we assumed that the X-ray machine had no salvage or residual value at the end of its 5-year life. If the machine had an estimated salvage value, it would have been discounted to the present and added to the present value of the labor savings.

2. Our example emphasized the quantitative financial aspects of the decision. Qualitative factors must also be considered. Will the new X-ray machine require more space? Will the new

machine be easier to operate? Will improved diagnoses result from the purchase of the new machine?

Present Value Index

The present value index (PVI), also referred to as the profitability index, is a modification of the NPV method. PVI can be used to compare even or uneven (not in the form of an annuity) investments in mutually exclusive projects (acceptance of one project automatically means rejection of the other). The PVI is the ratio of the present value of the cash inflows to the present value of the investment and is expressed as

$$PVI = \frac{\text{Present value of cash inflows}}{\text{Present value of the investment}}$$

Suppose a company wishes to invest in a word-processing software package for all of its operations. The company narrows its choices to software package A at $400,000 or software package B at $225,000. The following present values of the cash inflows have been calculated using a discount rate of 10 percent: $600,000 for software package A, and $350,000 for software package B. A comparison reveals the present value index.

	(a) Present Value of the Inflows	(b) Initial Investment	(a − b) Net Present Value	Present Value Index
Package A	$600,000	$400,000	$200,000	1.50
Package B	350,000	200,000	150,000	1.75

On the surface, the purchase of software package A seems to be the better investment because its NPV is larger; however, the PVI indicates that the purchase of software package B is a more efficient use of the company's assets (all other things being equal). The greater

PVI indicates a higher rate of return on software package B than on software package A.

In general, PVI provides better information than the NPV method in two situations:

1. Availability of funds is limited (capital is subject to rationing).

2. The projects are mutually exclusive.

Like the NPV method, the PVI method does not show the expected rate of return on the investment. However, in our example, we know that the expected rate of return is greater than 10 percent because the PVI is greater than 1.0. A PVI of 1.0 would indicate that the expected rate of return is exactly 10 percent.

Internal Rate of Return

The internal rate of return (IRR) is sometimes referred to as the time-adjusted rate of return. The IRR is the rate at which the present value of the inflows is equal to the present value of the outflows; that is, it is the rate that makes the NPV equal to zero. The IRR is compared to the required rate of return. If the IRR is higher than the required rate of return, the project is selected; if the required rate is lower, the project is rejected, because its expected rate of return is less than the company's required minimum rate. IRR rates higher than the minimum are preferred because they raise the company's ROI.

A financial calculator or computer program is usually used to determine the rate that equates the present value of the inflows with the present value of the outflows (NPV = $0). If a calculator or computer program is not available, a trial-and-error approach is used with the aid of an annuity table. For example, assume that a company is considering the purchase of a new machine that will result in labor savings of $10,000 a year for four years. The new machine will cost $29,140 and will have no salvage value at the end of its four-year life. To get the NPV of this investment, we calculate the present value of the inflows (labor savings) and compare that amount to the present value of the outflows (the initial investment). Referring to Table 16–3, we initially choose a discount rate of 10 percent and test the resulting figures.

Present value of the inflows (savings)	$10,000 × 3.170 = $31,700
Present value of the outflows (investment)	$29,140 × 1.0 = (29,140)
Net Present Value	$ 2,560

The NPV is positive, indicating that the expected rate of return on the proposal is greater than our chosen discount rate of 10 percent.

The relationship between the present value of the inflows and the present value of the outflows is:

$$\begin{array}{ccc} \text{Net present value} & \text{Net present value} & \text{Net present value} \\ \text{of the savings} & - \quad \text{of the investment} & = \quad \text{of the project} \end{array}$$

$$(\$10,000 \times 3.170) \ - \ (\$29,140 \times 1.0) \ = \ \$2,560$$

The equation indicates that:

$$\left(\begin{array}{c} \text{Annual after-tax} \\ \text{cash flow} \end{array} \times \begin{array}{c} \text{Interest table} \\ \text{factor} \end{array}\right) - \left(\begin{array}{c} \text{Initial} \\ \text{investment} \end{array}\right) = \text{NPV}$$

Because the IRR is the rate that equates the present value of the inflows with the present value of the outflows, we can set the NPV to zero in our equation.

$$(\$10,000 \times \ ?) - \$29,140 = \$0$$

Solving the equation for the interest factor results in:

$$\frac{\text{Initial investment}}{\text{Annual after-tax cash flow}} = \frac{\$29,140}{\$10,000} = 2.914$$

Returning to Table 16–3 and reading the row for four periods, we see that 2.914 would be 14 percent. We can state the IRR for this project as 14 percent and compare that result to the company's required rate of return. (This rate is the lowest rate of return that management will accept and is normally at least equal to the company's cost of capital.)

In our example, the after-tax cash flows are in the form of an annuity. If, instead, cash flows are uneven and a financial calculator or computer program is not available, each of the cash inflows must be discounted to the present so that their sum will be equal to the initial investment (NPV = \$0). This process is tedious and time-consuming when using the trial-and-error method. Finding the precise IRR of a project is difficult without a financial calculator or computer, because present value tables normally do not provide factors for fractional interest rates.

19

PAYBACK AND ACCOUNTING RATE OF RETURN

Net present value, the present value index, and the internal rate of return—all capital budgeting approaches that consider the time value of money—are discussed in Chapter 18. The two project selection methods that do not discount cash flows—the payback method and the accounting rate of return—are not as useful in evaluating investment projects as the discounted cash flow methods. However, they are easy to use and provide practical information.

Payback Method

The payback method is one of the simplest and most widely used approaches to evaluating capital investment projects. The method is employed in the capital budgeting process by Fortune 500 giants and small mom-and-pop companies alike.

The payback period is the length of time required to recoup the original investment through the investment's cash flows. For example, if a project requires an initial investment of $250,000 and will generate cash flows of $50,000 per year for eight years, the payback period is five years ($250,000/$50,000). If the cash flow of a project is an annuity, the payback period is determined as follows.

$$\text{Payback period} = \frac{\text{Initial investment}}{\text{Cash flow per year}}$$

If a second project had an initial investment of $527,869 and the cash flows were $75,000 for 16 years, the payback period for this project is 7.04 years.

The payback period focuses on the timing of cash flows to measure project risk; that is, the farther away cash flows are, the more uncertain is their receipt. Conversely, current or relatively current cash flows have less risk. The assumption is that the longer the time to recoup the original investment, the greater the project's risk. A shorter payback period allows the company to recover its investment faster and enables it to reinvest those funds in other projects.

Expanded Example

Assume that Morgan Company is planning to expand by constructing a new factory. Morgan estimates that when the factory is operational, it will generate additional sales of $275,000 for each of the next 10 years. The new factory will cost $600,000 to build and will have a life of 10 years with no salvage value. Depreciation expense is computed using the straight-line method. Additional operating costs associated with the new plant (including depreciation expense) are estimated to be $180,000. Morgan's income tax rate is 30 percent. Projections for the project are shown in the following income statement.

Morgan Company
Income Statement

Additional sales	$275,000
Less: Additional operating expenses (including depreciation of $60,000)	180,000
Income before income taxes	95,000
Income tax expense at 30%	28,500
Net income	$ 66,500

The new factory will increase net income by $66,500; however, net income is an accrual concept, and payback focuses on cash flows. Therefore, the $66,500 net income figure must be adjusted for noncash depreciation expense. Adding the depreciation expense to net income arrives at after-tax cash flows from operations of $126,500 ($66,500 + $60,000). The resulting payback period is almost four and three-quarters years:

$$\frac{\text{Original investment}}{\text{After-tax cash flow per year}} = \text{Payback period}$$

$$\frac{\$600,000}{\$126,500} = 4.74 \text{ years}$$

In this example, the after-tax cash flows are the actual cash flows, because additional sales have exceeded additional operating expenses. The calculation of the payback period is exactly the same if we instead have an investment that reduces expenses and results in a savings. In this case, divide the initial investment by the annual after-tax cash savings that resulted from the reduced cash outflow.

Unequal Cash Flows

Our previous examples have assumed that the annual after-tax cash flows resulting from each of the projects are annuities (the same amount for each year of the project's life). Now consider a project costing $80,000 that has the following after-tax cash flows:

Year	After-Tax Cash Flows
1	$12,000
2	8,000
3	16,000
4	18,000
5	19,000
6	17,000
7	11,000
8	13,000

Here, we determine the payback period by calculating the yearly cumulative total of cash flows until the total exceeds the initial investment.

Year	Amount	Cumulative Total
1	$12,000	$12,000
2	8,000	20,000
3	16,000	36,000
4	18,000	54,000
5	19,000	73,000
6	17,000	90,000

The complete payback occurs in the sixth year. Because $73,000 will be received by the end of the fifth year, $7,000 more is needed to recoup the original investment of $80,000. If the $17,000 cash inflow in the sixth year occurs evenly throughout the year, it will take 0.4118 percent ($7,000/$17,000) of the sixth year to recover the remainder of the original investment. This results in a payback period of approximately 5 years and 5 months (0.4118 × 12 months).

Payback Reciprocal

The payback method can be used to approximate the rate of return on a capital investment project when the following two conditions are met:

1. The annual after-tax cash flows are expected to occur evenly (as an annuity) over the life of the project.

2. The estimated useful life of the capital investment project is at least twice the payback period.

In the Morgan Company example, the payback period is 4.74 years, and the estimated life of the project is 10 years. The estimated after-tax cash flows occur uniformly. Using the payback reciprocal, we determine that the rate of return is 21 percent.

$$\frac{1}{\text{Payback period}} = \text{Payback reciprocal}$$

$$\frac{1}{4.74} = 0.211$$

If the life of the project is interminable, the payback reciprocal results in the exact rate of return on the proposed capital investment project. If the life of the project is finite, the payback reciprocal provides a rate that is somewhat higher than the exact rate.

Limitations of the Payback Method

The payback method has the following four limitations:

1. The method stresses return *of* investment and does not consider return *on* investment. An investment with a longer payback period may be more profitable and therefore may be superior to one with a shorter payback period.

2. The payback period ignores cash flows after the payback period. For example, assume the following information for projects B and L:

	Project B	*Project L*
Initial investment	$75,000	$75,000
Annual after-tax cash flows	$15,000	$ 7,500
Life of project	6 years	15 years

Project B's payback is five years and Project L's is ten years. On this basis, Project B appears to be the superior project; however, Project L may actually be the better investment because its cash inflows continue for five years after the payback period. Project B's cash inflows continue for only one additional year.

3. The method ignores the time value of money.

4. The method ignores the timing of cash flows.

Regarding timing, suppose two projects had the following cash flows:

	Project A	*Project Z*
Initial investment	$30,000	$30,000
Cash flows:		
Year 1	15,000	2,000
Year 2	9,000	3,000
Year 3	6,000	25,000
Year 4	3,000	9,000
Year 5	2,000	6,000
Year 6	25,000	15,000

For both projects the total cash flows are the same ($60,000) and the payback period is three years. However, the cash flow from Project A recovered the investment at a faster rate, compared to Project Z. Therefore, Project A should be selected. If two projects have the same total cash flows, select the one that accumulates cash the fastest and recovers the initial investment in the shortest period of time. The payback method does not take this into consideration.

Because of its limitations, the payback method should not be used as the primary investment evaluation tool. However, many companies use the payback method as a screening tool in their investment evaluation process. Projects that meet the maximum acceptable payback period are then subjected to evaluation by other capital budgeting techniques.

Accounting Rate of Return

The accounting rate of return (ARR) is a measure of profitability that associates the expected average return with the project investment base. The numerator is normally the expected annual earnings from the project, and the denominator is the average investment or, in some cases, the initial investment. The ARR method uses projected earnings based on accrual-based financial statements rather than on cash flows. The general formula for ARR is:

$$\frac{\text{Average annual expected earnings}}{\text{Average investment}} = ARR$$

ARR sometimes is called the book value method, financial statement method, unadjusted rate of return method, or rate of return on assets method.

The numerator consists of the average difference between revenues and expenses resulting from the proposed project. Expenses may include income taxes and depreciation. There is disagreement among accountants as to whether some expenses (e.g., depreciation, and research and development) should be included because of their long-term nature, and whether operating income or net earnings should be used to determine profitability.

The denominator is either the initial investment or the average investment. The average investment is calculated by adding the initial investment plus the value of the investment at the end of the project's life, and dividing the sum by 2. The use of the initial investment can be supported by the fact that it does not change over time (it is not affected by depreciation expense) and thus allows an easy comparison to the actual rate of return obtained. Because the use of initial investment ignores the return of funds at the end of the project's life, average investment is sometimes used.

Calculation of ARR

To illustrate the computation of the accounting rate of return, assume that information regarding two pieces of machinery is being considered by X Company. The company uses straight-line depreciation and has an income tax rate of 30 percent.

	Machine A	Machine B
Initial investment	$150,000	$120,000
Estimated salvage value on machinery	15,000	0
Amount subject to depreciation	$135,000	$120,000
Estimated useful life	10 years	8 years
Annual amount of depreciation expense	$ 13,500	$ 15,000
Estimated annual average earnings before depreciation and income taxes	$ 25,000	$ 22,000
Less: Depreciation expense	13,500	15,000
Estimated annual average earnings after depreciation and before income taxes	11,500	7,000
Income taxes at 30%	3,450	2,100
Estimated annual average earnings	$ 8,050	$ 4,900
Average investment	$ 82,500[a]	$ 60,000[b]
ARR	9.8%[c]	8.1%[d]

[a] ($150,000 + $15,000)/2
[b] ($120,000 + $0)/2
[c] $8,050/$82,500
[d] $4,900/$60,000

The analysis indicates that Machine A is expected to result in a higher ARR than Machine B, even though Machine A has a higher initial investment. Additionally, the resulting ARRs can be compared with the company's preestablished hurdle rate or cost of capital.

ARR is simple to calculate and easily understood. The ARR from one project can be compared to other investment opportunities. If the objective of capital budgeting is to increase company ROI, then the use of ARR as an evaluative tool is consistent with that objective.

Limitations of ARR

Several limitations are associated with the use of ARR as an investment evaluation tool. They include the following:

√ 1. ARR focuses only on accounting earnings and ignores cash flows.

√ 2. ARR ignores the time value of money. In other words, the method values earnings to be realized in future periods in the same manner as earnings realized today.

√ 3. The use of accrual-based amounts may not be appropriate for capital budgeting decisions. For example, costs such as research and development and advertising costs benefit future periods but are normally charged to expense in the period incurred. These items might be more appropriately classified as part of the investment base rather than deducted in arriving at estimated annual average earnings. The use of accrual-based amounts with adjustment for items of this nature might lead to an erroneous ARR calculation that would affect the possible selection or rejection of a proposed investment project.

√ 4. ARR ignores the timing of cash flows; that is, the method ignores how quickly cash flows are recovered.

√ 5. ARR ignores the total profitability of a project. A project that returns 15 percent for 5 years has the same ARR as a project that returns 15 percent for 50 years.

20

COMPARISON OF CAPITAL
BUDGETING METHODS

Most financial managers believe that, compared to payback and the accounting rate of return, discounted cash flow methods are conceptually appealing and superior capital investment analysis tools. However, managers should be aware of the similarities and differences of the various methods, as well as their underlying assumptions and limitations. This understanding allows managers to use several capital budgeting techniques simultaneously to evaluate a project or projects. This chapter discusses the assumptions, advantages, and limitations of each of these methods.

Nondiscounted Methods

Payback

Assumptions. The payback method assumes that the size and the timing of cash flows can be accurately predicted. The primary consideration under this method is the speed at which the investment can be recouped. Projects with shorter payback periods are preferred over those with longer payback periods because they are assumed to bear less risk.

Advantages. Many managers select projects with a short payback period because these projects are more liquid than projects with longer payback periods. The payback method emphasizes liquidity and allows managers greater flexibility in planning for the availability of funds. The method is easy to use and understand, and it can be useful as a project planning tool, especially when a project's continuation is uncertain. A company investing in Libya might be very interested in how its capital is at risk.

Limitations.   The payback method ignores the time value of money and cash flows after the payback period. The method does not give consideration to management's preferences regarding the timing of cash flows. Also, the method results in a singular measure (the payback period) rather than a range of values. Finally, the method neglects the profitability of the project.

Accounting Rate of Return (ARR)

Assumptions.   ARR assumes that there is a direct relationship between accounting earnings and investment. It is the one method not based on cash flows. The method also assumes that the projected timing, size, and direction of accounting earnings can be accurately predicted. Average investment, residual value (if any), and project life are also assumed to be reasonably predictable.

Advantages.   ARR is simple and easy to understand; unlike the payback method, ARR considers profitability. The resulting measure is easily comparable to a required rate of return when choosing among investment projects.

Limitations.   The ARR method does not consider cash flows or the time value of money. This method also results in only one measure, without consideration of probabilities.

Discounted Cash Flow Measures

One general assumption we make in Chapter 18, which relates to all three discounted cash flow methods, is that all cash flows from an investment occur at the end of the time period. In reality, most cash flows occur *throughout* a period. Treating after-tax cash flows as if they have occurred in the pattern of an annuity simplifies calculations; however, you should be aware that this assumption increases the variability in the resulting estimate of the rate or amount if in fact the actual cash flows do not occur in this pattern.

A second general assumption of discounted cash flow analysis is that a company is able to reinvest the cash returns from a project at a rate of return equal to the discount rate. Unless the company can actually earn that rate, the real rate of return on the project is overstated. For example, if the discount rate used to evaluate a project is 14 percent, discounted cash flow analysis assumes the cash returns from the project can be invested in another project that has a 14 percent rate of return. If the company finds that the other project has a rate of return of only 11 percent, the real rate on the initial project will be less than 14 percent. This assumption can lead managers to make the wrong decision regarding the acceptance, rejection, or ranking of a particular project. This assumption is especially critical when all projects do not have the same estimated lives.

Present Value Index (PVI)

Assumptions. PVI assumes that the timing and size of cash flows and project life can be accurately predicted. This method assumes that the key consideration is the relationship between the present value of the net cash inflows and the present value of the investment as a measure of efficient capital utilization. The discount rate is assumed to be valid.

Advantages. PVI is simple and easy to understand, provides better information than net present value when projects are mutually exclusive and available investment funds are limited. PVI considers cash flow and the time value of money.

Limitations. Management's preference for cash flow patterns are ignored. PVI results in a single measure without considerations of a probabilistic range, such as optimistic, most likely, or pessimistic estimates. This method does not result in a dollar figure or a rate of return.

Net Present Value (NPV)

Assumptions. The timing and size of cash flows and the project life are assumed to be predictable. The discount rate used in the analysis is also assumed to be valid.

Advantages. NPV takes into consideration cash flows and the time value of money. Although NPV does not result in a rate of return, it does provide information on whether the actual rate of return is higher or lower than, or equal to, the required rate of return. The method is most effective when it is used to select the best project among competing projects (when all have approximately the same initial investment cost).

Limitations. NPV does not explicitly produce a project rate of return or generate an internal rate of return. Project rankings are based on total dollars, and probabilities of actual results are not considered. When independent projects do not have approximately the same original cost, NPV should not be used because such comparisons favor projects with higher NPVs without considering the initial investment. NPV does not explicitly consider a range of values.

Internal Rate of Return (IRR)

Assumptions. IRR assumes that the timing and size of cash flows and project life can be accurately predicted, and that the minimum required rate of return is valid.

Advantages. Results can easily be compared to a minimum or required rate of return. IRR takes into consideration cash flows and the time value of money.

Limitations. Multiple rates of return on the same project are possible under this method when certain patterns of cash flow exist. IRR does not use probabilities to consider a range of values. IRR ranks projects by rates of return rather than dollars.

Comparison of Net Present Value and Internal Rate of Return

The NPV method is easier to apply than IRR when cash flows are not in the pattern of an annuity. But the NPV method requires one piece of information that the IRR does not—the selection of an appropriate discount rate to be used in calculating the present value of the cash flows. Accountants do not agree on the appropriate manner of calculating this rate; it may be the company's weighted average cost of capital, a target rate set by management, or some other rate. The choice of the rate has a significant impact on the calculation of NPV.

The IRR method has the advantage of not requiring a discount rate for making the calculation. The resulting IRR percentage is easily compared to other rates of return.

One weakness of the IRR method is that it is difficult to compute when after-tax cash flows are not uniform from year to year. Also, when cash flows are not uniform, it is possible that more than one IRR will result in a net present value of zero, making the evaluation of a project very difficult. NPV always results in a unique answer. Because IRR is a percentage, the combined IRRs of a group of projects have little meaning. However, because NPV is in dollars, not a percentage, we can add NPVs of independent projects to determine the effect of a combination of investment projects.

When the discount rate is not constant for all years of a proposed investment project, NPV can still be used by calculating a present value of the cash flow for each year to determine a total net present value. The use of different discount rates for each year of a project means that there is no one figure that the IRR can be compared to when making

211

EXHIBIT 20-1
NPV with Different Target Rates of Return

Year	Cash Flow	Required Rate of Return (%)	Present Value of $1 Discounted at the Target Rate of Return	Present Value of Cash Inflows
1	$50,000	8	0.926	$ 46,300
2	50,000	8	0.857	42,850
3	50,000	12	0.712	35,600
4	50,000	14	0.592	29,600
5	50,000	16	0.476	23,800
				$178,150

a decision to accept or reject a project. For example, management's target rate of return for the next five years may be 8 percent for the first two years, and 12 percent, 14 percent, and 16 percent, respectively, for the following three years. Cash flows for each of the five years is $50,000 and the initial investment is $181,300. In considering a five-year project, a NPV can be calculated using a different rate to discount cash flows each year. Exhibit 20–1 presents the analysis of this project. The project is not attractive with a negative NPV of $3,150. But what of IRR? Is an IRR of 15 percent acceptable, or must it exceed 16 percent for the total project? The decision is not clear. IRR cannot be used to determine whether the project should be accepted or rejected. Finally, sensitivity analysis allows us to use changes in the investment data as a way of measuring how much the decision has changed. We can vary the discount rate and calculate a whole set of NPVs to see whether our initial decision is affected. IRR is difficult to use for sensitivity analysis because it cannot be adjusted to reflect different discount rates.

21

IMPORTANT ROI RATIOS

*F*inancial statements serve many users, inside and outside a company. This chapter described ratios that are used to assess the financial health and earning power of a company. These ratios are helpful in making investment decisions, such as whether to buy, sell, or hold stocks and bonds; on whether to extend or deny loans or trade credit. The financial statements (balance sheet, income statement, and statement of cash flows) provide much of the information needed for making these investment decisions.

Investment Decisions

The principal purpose of financial analysis is to form judgments about the future. Will the company be able to repay a short-term bank loan, or a 20-year bond? Will the company's income and ROI increase? Is the dividend payment likely to rise? Is the market price of the stock too high or too low? In arriving at answers to these questions, we work primarily with historical information and assume, unless there is other evidence to the contrary, that the historical trends will continue. However, a company might be negatively impacted by some event beyond its control. A competitor could come out with a superior product, or a strike might result in lost sales. In evaluating a company, we must watch for developments that might make the future different from the past. Also, because good management is vital to a company's success, one of the major questions that we seek to answer is whether the managers are running the company in the most efficient and effective manner.

Financial statement analysis also focuses on nonfinancial, qualitative information. Other sources of information that assist in financial statement analysis are the financial press (for example, the *Wall Street Journal*), reports to the Securities and Exchange Commission, and business service publications such as *Value Line* and various Dun & Bradstreet products.

The focus in this chapter is on the financial and quantitative information contained in a company's financial statements relating to ROI. We apply our analysis to a set of published financial statements and examine significant relationships.

Ratio Analysis

Although there are other aspects to financial analysis, the calculation and interpretation of financial ratios is one of the most prominent. Ratios by themselves reveal little. In order to be of value, ratios must be compared to each other or to benchmarks or norms. Common benchmarks are average ratios for the industry in which the company operates, values that the analyst considers good or bad, and values for the same company in previous years. Four areas are of interest to investors because of their effect on the decisions investors make:

1. Liquidity.
2. Activity.
3. Solvency.
4. Profitability.

This book is concerned with profitability—the company's capacity to generate profits.

Keep two important points in mind: (1) the computation of a company's ratios is only a starting point in an analysis, because ratios give only signs, not answers, as to what might be expected; and (2) ratios can give conflicting signals. For instance, the more cash a company has, the better its ability to pay its debts; however, having excess cash is not always a good strategy because the company might realize higher income if it invested the excess cash wisely. This type of paradox recurs throughout financial statement analysis.

Profitability

Stockholders have the most difficult analytical task. They are concerned with profitability, earnings, dividends, and increases in the market price of a company's shares. Ratios relating to these areas are presented and discussed in later sections of this chapter.

Illustrative Financial Statements

The income statement and balance sheets and some additional financial information from the 1994 annual report of Coca-Cola Company (Exhibit 21–1) serve as examples for discussion.

Income Statement Ratios

The income statement has at least three important ratios that assist the user in assessing a company's earning power. The first is the gross profit ratio (gross profit divided by net sales revenue). The second is the operating ratio (operating income divided by net sales revenue). The third is return on sales (ROS) (net income divided by net sales revenue). These ratios for Coca-Cola Company in 1994 are 61.9 percent, 22.9 percent, and 15.8 percent, respectively. The gross profit ratio decreased slightly in 1994, compared to 1993, but the operating ratio and ROS remained relatively stable.

EXHIBIT 21–1
Consolidated Statements of Income for the
Coca-Cola Company and Subsidiaries

Year Ended December 31,	1994	1993	1992
(In millions except per share data)			
Net Operating Revenues	$16,172	$13,957	$13,074
Cost of goods sold	6,167	5,160	5,055
Gross Profit	10,005	8,797	8,019
Selling, administrative and general expenses	6,297	5,695	5,249
Operating Income	3,708	3,102	2,770
Interest income	181	144	164
Interest expense	199	168	171
Equity income	134	91	65
Other income (deductions)—net	(96)	4	(82)
Gain on issuance of stock by Coca-Cola Amatil	—	12	—
Income before Income Taxes and Changes in Accounting Principles	3,728	3,185	2,746
Income taxes	1,174	997	863
Income before Changes in Accounting Principles	2,554	2,188	1,883
Transition effects of changes in accounting principles			
Postemployment benefits	—	(12)	—
Postretirement benefits other than pensions			
Consolidated operations	—	—	(146)
Equity investments	—	—	(73)
Net Income	$ 2,554	$ 2,176	$ 1,664
Income per Share			
Before changes in accounting principles	$ 1.98	$ 1.68	$ 1.43
Transition effects of changes in accounting principles			
Postemployment benefits	—	(.01)	—
Postretirement benefits other than pensions			
Consolidated operations	—	—	(.11)
Equity investments	—	—	(.06)
Net Income per Share	$ 1.98	$ 1.67	$ 1.26
Average Shares Outstanding	1,290	1,302	1,317

(continued)

EXHIBIT 21–1 (continued)
Quarterly Data (Unaudited) for the
Coca-Cola Company and Subsidiaries

Year Ended December 31,	First Quarter	Second Quarter	Third Quarter	Fourth Quarter	Full Year
(In millions except per share data)					
1994					
Net operating revenues	$3,352	$4,342	$4,461	$4,017	$16,172
Gross profit	2,110	2,675	2,701	2,519	10,005
Net income	521	758	708	567	2,554
Net income per share	.40	.59	.55	.44	1.98
1993[1]					
Net operating revenues	$3,056	$3,899	$3,629	$3,373	$13,957
Gross profit	1,963	2,435	2,286	2,113	8,797
Income before change in accounting principle	454	678	590	466	2,188
Net income	442	678	590	466	2,176
Income per share before change in accounting principle	.35	.52	.45	.36	1.68
Net income per share	.34	.52	.45	.36	1.67

[1] The first quarter of 1993 included an after-tax transition charge of $12 million ($.01 per share) related to the change in accounting for postemployment benefits. The third quarter of 1993 included an after-tax impact of $47 million due to changes in U.S. tax law which reduced full year after-tax income by $51 million ($.04 per share) and the reversal of previously recorded reserves for bottler litigation of $23 million ($.01 per share after income taxes). The fourth quarter of 1993 included provisions to increase efficiencies of $63 million ($.03 per share after income taxes), a reduction of $42 million ($.02 per share after income taxes) related to restructuring charges recorded by an equity investee, a gain from the sale of real estate in Japan ($34 million, or $.02 per share after income taxes), a gain from the sale of citrus groves in the United States ($50 million, or $.02 per share after income taxes) and a gain recognized on the issuance of stock by an equity investee of $12 million ($.01 per share after income taxes).

Stock Prices

Below are the New York Stock Exchange high, low, and closing prices of The Coca-Cola Company's stock for each quarter of 1994 and 1993.

	First Quarter	Second Quarter	Third Quarter	Fourth Quarter
1994				
High	$44.75	$42.38	$50.00	$53.50
Low	40.13	38.88	41.00	48.00
Close	40.63	40.63	48.63	51.50
1993				
High	$44.13	$43.63	$44.75	$45.13
Low	40.00	37.50	41.75	40.00
Close	42.63	43.00	42.25	44.63

(continued)

EXHIBIT 21–1 (continued)
Consolidated Balance Sheets for the
Coca-Cola Company and Subsidiaries

December 31,	1994	1993
(In millions except share data)		
Assets		
Current		
Cash and cash equivalents	$ 1,386	$ 998
Marketable securities	145	80
	1,531	1,078
Trade accounts receivable, less allowances of $33		
in 1994 and $39 in 1993	1,470	1,210
Finance subsidiary receivables	55	33
Inventories	1,047	1,049
Prepaid expenses and other assets	1,102	1,064
Total Current Assets	5,205	4,434
Investments and Other Assets		
Equity method investments		
Coca-Cola Enterprises Inc.	524	498
Coca-Cola Amatil Limited	694	592
Other, principally bottling companies	1,114	1,037
Cost method investments, principally		
bottling companies	178	88
Finance subsidiary receivables	255	226
Marketable securities and other assets	1,163	868
	3,928	3,309
Property, Plant and Equipment		
Land	221	197
Buildings and improvements	1,814	1,616
Machinery and equipment	3,776	3,380
Containers	346	403
	6,157	5,596
Less allowances for depreciation	2,077	1,867
	4,080	3,729
Goodwill and Other Intangible Assets	660	549
	$13,873	$12,021

(continued)

EXHIBIT 21–1 (continued)

December 31,	1994	1993
(In millions except share data)		
Liabilities and Share-Owners' Equity		
Current		
Accounts payable and accrued expenses	$ 2,564	$ 2,217
Loans and notes payable	1,757	1,409
Finance subsidiary notes payable	291	244
Current maturities of long-term debt	35	19
Accrued taxes	1,530	1,282
Total Current Liabilities	6,177	5,171
Long-Term Debt	1,426	1,428
Other Liabilities	855	725
Deferred Income Taxes	180	113
Share-Owners' Equity		
Common stock, $.25 par value		
Authorized: 2,800,000,000 shares		
Issued: 1,707,627,955 shares in 1994;		
1,703,526,299 shares in 1993	427	426
Capital surplus	1,173	1,086
Reinvested earnings	11,006	9,458
Unearned compensation related to outstanding		
restricted stock	(74)	(85)
Foreign currency translation adjustment	(272)	(420)
Unrealized gain on securities available-for-sale	48	—
	12,308	10,465
Less treasury stock, at cost (431,694,661		
shares in 1994;		
406,072,817 shares in 1993)	7,073	5,881
	5,235	4,584
	$13,873	$12,021

(continued)

EXHIBIT 21–1 (continued)
Consolidated Statements of Shareowners' Equity for the
Coca-Cola Company and Subsidiaries

Three Years Ended December 31, 1994	Number of Common Shares Outstanding	Common Stock	Capital Surplus
(In millions except per share data)			
Balance December 31, 1991	1,329	$422	$ 640
Stock issues to employees exercising stock options	9	2	129
Tax benefit from employees' stock option and restricted stock plans	—	—	93
Stock issued under restricted stock plans, less amortization of $25	—	—	9
Translation adjustments	—	—	—
Purchases of stock for treasury	(31)[1]	—	—
Net income	—	—	—
Dividends (per share—$.56)	—	—	—
Balance December 31, 1992	1,307	424	871
Stock issued to employees exercising stock options	7	2	143
Tax benefit from employees' stock option and restricted stock plans	—	—	66
Stock issued under restricted stock plans, less amortization of $19	—	—	6
Translation adjustments	—	—	—
Purchases of stock for treasury	(17)[1]	—	—
Net income	—	—	—
Dividends (per share—$.68)	—	—	—
Balance, December 31, 1993	1,297	426	1,086
Transition effect of change in accounting for certain debt and marketable equity securities, net of deferred taxes	—	—	—
Stock issued to employees exercising stock options	4	1	68
Tax benefit from employees' stock option and restricted stock plans	—	—	17
Stock issued under restricted stock plans, less amortization of $13	—	—	2
Translation adjustments	—	—	—
Net change in unrealized gain on securities, net of deferred taxes	—	—	—
Purchases of stock for treasury	(25)[1]	—	—
Net income	—	—	—
Dividends (per share—$.78)	—	—	—
Balance December 31, 1994	1,276	$427	$1,173

[1]Common stock purchased from employees exercising stock options amounted to 208 thousand, 2.7 million, and 1.3 million shares for the years ending December 31, 1994, 1993, and 1992, respectively

Reinvested Earnings	Outstanding Restricted Stock	Foreign Currency Translation	Unrealized Gain on Securities	Treasury Stock
$ 7,239	$(115)	$ (5)	$—	$(3,942)
—	—	—	—	—
—	—	—	—	—
—	15	—	—	—
—	—	(266)	—	—.
—	—	—	—	(1,259)
1,664	—	—	—	—
(738)	—	—	—	—
8,165	(100)	(271)	—	(5,201)
—	—	—	—	—
—	—	—	—	—
—	15	—	—	—
—	—	(149)	—	—
—	—	—	—	(680)
2,176	—	—	—	—
(883)	—	—	—	—
9,458	(85)	(420)	—	(5,881)
—	—	—	60	—
—	—	—	—	—
—	—	—	—	—
—	11	—	—	—
—	—	148	—	—
—	—	—	(12)	—
—	—	—	—	(1,192)
2,554	—	—	—	—
(1,006)	—	—	—	—
$11,006	$ (74)	$(272)	$48	$(7,073)

These ratios are primarily concerned with profitability and provide clues to the efficiency of operations, that is, how well the company's managers were able to turn each dollar in sales into gross profit, operating profit, and net income. A number of conclusions can be drawn from these ratios, depending on the results. For example, if a company has a gross profit ratio that is high compared to some norm, but its operating ratio is low, we might conclude that the company is using a high-price, high-promotion strategy. A high gross profit ratio indicates either higher selling prices or lower cost of goods sold. A low operating ratio with a high gross profit ratio indicates relatively high operating expenses, such as advertising and promotion. Other explanations are possible, and a great deal more work is necessary before any conclusions can be reached.

Balance Sheet Ratios

Balance sheet ratios are usually less important than income statement ratios, and are normally used only to spot trends in particular asset and liability categories. For example, inventories might be increasing at a faster rate than receivables and cash, indicating that the company is holding slow-moving goods and might need to reduce prices to sell its inventory and stay competitive.

Profitability Ratios

Return on Investment

Profitability is normally measured in dollars of net income or by ratios. The most common measure of profitability is return on investment (ROI).

$$\frac{\text{Income}}{\text{Investment}} = \text{Return on investment (ROI)}$$

Most measures of ROI relate an income statement element (such as operating or net income) to a balance sheet element (such as stockholders' equity). Stockholders and potential stockholders are interested in the return they might expect to receive from their investment, and company managers are concerned with earning satisfactory returns on the assets under their control. This is why, as we explain throughout this book, different users define income and investment differently when measuring ROI.

Return on Assets

The return on assets (ROA) ratio measures operating efficiency and is used for investment centers. This ratio provides evidence as to how well company managers are using the assets they control to generate income. The most common calculation of the ratio is as follows.

$$\frac{\text{Operating income}}{\text{Average total assets}} = \text{Return on assets (ROA)}$$

For Coca-Cola Company, ROA was almost 29 percent for 1994, calculated as follows:

$$\frac{\$3,708,000,000}{(\$13,873,000,000 + \$12,021,000,000)/2} = .286 = 28.6\%$$

The most common measure of average total assets is the sum of the beginning and ending balance sheet amounts, divided by 2. Significant month-to-month fluctuations are less likely with total assets than with current assets such as receivables and inventory. Average total assets is used in the calculation, because the numerator (income) is earned continuously throughout the year. Some users replace average assets with end-of-year assets in the denominator, and others use beginning-of-year amounts. Still others use total assets minus current liabilities because, they argue, this formula provides a stable source of financing that directly relates to operations.

Return on Equity (ROE)

Common stockholders are concerned about the return on *their* investment. That return depends not only on profitable operations, but also on the amount of debt and preferred stock in the capital structure.

Return on equity (ROE) is computed as follows.

$$\frac{\text{Net income}}{\text{Average common stockholders' equity}} = \text{ROE}$$

For a company such as Coca-Cola, with no preferred stock, average common stockholders' equity is the sum of the beginning and ending amounts of stockholders' equity divided by 2. For a company that has outstanding preferred stock, preferred dividends must be subtracted from net income in the numerator, and the amount of total stockholders' equity attributable to preferred stock must be subtracted from total stockholders' equity in the denominator to obtain common stockholders' equity. ROE for Coca-Cola Company in 1994 is 52 percent, figured as follows.

$$\frac{\$2,554,000,000}{(\$5,235,000,000 + \$4,584,000,000)/2} = .52 = 52\%$$

Creditors receive interest, a fixed amount, and do not receive any amount beyond interest even if the company is very profitable. If ROA is greater than the interest rate a company pays to its creditors, the company can increase ROE by using debt. Using debt to increase ROE is called leverage or trading on the equity. However, because debt is increased, leverage increases the risk to stockholders.

Earnings per Share

Investors generally buy shares in a company and focus on per-share data. Earnings per share (EPS) is the most widely reported statistic in the financial press and in recommendations by investment services. In its simplest form, EPS is calculated as follows.

$$\frac{\text{Net income available for common stockholders}}{\text{Weighted-average common shares outstanding}} = \text{Earnings per share (EPS)}$$

(Complicating factors relating to earnings per share are beyond the scope of this book.) Because preferred stockholders have first claim to dividends, preferred stock dividends are subtracted from net income to arrive at the earnings available to the common stockholders. The weighted-average number of common shares outstanding is the best measure of shares outstanding throughout the period. Exhibit 21–1 indicates that Coca-Cola Company had 1,290 million shares outstanding at the end of 1994 and 1,302 million shares outstanding at the end of 1993. Coca-Cola's EPS is figured as follows.

$$1994: \frac{\$2,554,000,000 - \$0}{1,290,000,000 \text{ shares}} = \$1.98$$

$$1993: \frac{\$2,176,000,000 - \$0}{1,302,000,000 \text{ shares}} = \$1.67$$

Growth Rate of Earnings per Share

Coca-Cola's EPS in 1994 was $0.31 higher than in 1993. This is a growth rate of almost 19 percent, which can be calculated as follows.

$$\frac{\text{EPS current year} - \text{EPS prior year}}{\text{EPS prior year}} = \text{Growth rate of EPS}$$

$$\frac{\$1.98 - \$1.67}{\$1.67} = 0.186 = 18.6\%$$

The growth rate of EPS is useful because, generally, the higher the growth rate investors expect from a company, the more they are willing to pay for its stock. One caution: growth rates should be viewed over a number of years, not just a single year, because growth must be maintained to be meaningful.

Price–Earnings Ratio

The price–earnings (PE) ratio is the market price of a share of common stock divided by its earnings per share (EPS).

$$\frac{\text{Market price per share}}{\text{Earnings per share}} = \text{Price–earnings ratio}$$

This ratio is an important factor in decisions to buy, hold, or sell shares of stock, and is reported in the financial press. The PE ratio is the amount an investor is willing to pay for one dollar of earnings. High-growth companies normally have high PE ratios, and low-growth, stable, or declining companies have low ones. Exhibit 21–1 indicates that Coca-Cola's common stock sold at $51.50 per share at the end of 1994 and $44.63 at the end of 1993. The PE ratios are as follows.

$$1994: \frac{\$51.50}{\$1.98} = 26.0$$

$$1993: \frac{\$44.63}{\$1.67} = 26.7$$

A common stockholder's return on investment consists of two elements: (1) dividends, and (2) share appreciation. If investors' expectations are that a stock's earnings and dividends will increase, they are likely to be willing to pay more for that stock. The PE ratio focuses on both of these factors. To illustrate, if the market price of Smith Company stock is $50 and the market price of Jones Company stock is $30, you might think that Smith's stock is worth more than Jones's. You might also conclude that Smith Company is doing better than Jones Company. However, if the EPS figures for Smith Company and Jones Company are $6.50 and $1.95, respectively, we see that the PE ratios are as follows.

$$\text{Smith Company: } \frac{\$50.00}{\$6.50} = 7.7$$

$$\text{Jones Company: } \frac{\$30.00}{\$1.95} = 15.4$$

The PE ratios indicate that stockholders' expectations regarding growth in earnings and dividends are higher for Jones Company than for Smith Company. Apparently, investors are willing to pay much more for a dollar of earnings from Jones Company than for the same amount from Smith Company.

Dividend Yield

Investors receive dividends and, they hope, share price appreciation. The dividend yield, a measure of the percentage of market value that is paid annually in dividends, is calculated as follows:

$$\frac{\text{Dividend per share}}{\text{Market price per share}} = \text{Dividend yield}$$

Coca-Cola Company declared and paid dividends of $738,000,000 in 1994 and $883,000,000 in 1993, resulting in dividends per share of $0.56 and $0.58 for 1994 and 1993, respectively. With the share prices of $51.50 and $44.63 at the ends of 1994 and 1993, dividend yields are as follows:

$$1994: \frac{\$.56}{\$51.50} = 0.0101 = 1.01\%$$

$$1993: \frac{\$.58}{\$44.63} = 0.013 = 1.30\%$$

Investors normally compare dividend yields to other investment opportunities. They will usually accept lower yields from companies that reinvest earnings back into operations. The expectation is that reinvestment will lead to increased earnings and dividends in the future. Investors who favor growth companies are not as interested in dividends as they are in share appreciation of their stock. Because increases may not occur, investment in a high-growth company is generally riskier than investment in a mature company that pays relatively high, stable dividends.

EXHIBIT 21–2
Summary of Ratios

Income Statement Ratios

$$\text{Gross profit ratio} = \frac{\text{Gross profit}}{\text{Net sales}}$$

$$\text{Operating ratio} = \frac{\text{Operating income}}{\text{Net sales}}$$

$$\text{Return on sales} = \frac{\text{Net income}}{\text{Net sales}}$$

Profitability Ratios

$$\text{Return on investment} = \frac{\text{Income}}{\text{Investment}}$$

$$\text{Return on assets} = \frac{\text{Operating income}}{\text{Average total assets}}$$

$$\text{Return on Equity (ROE)} = \frac{\text{Net income}}{\text{Average common stockholders' equity}}$$

$$\frac{\text{Earnings}}{\text{per share}} = \frac{\text{Net income available for common stockholders}}{\text{Weighted-average common shares outstanding}}$$

$$\frac{\text{Growth rate of}}{\text{earnings per share}} = \frac{\text{EPS current year} - \text{EPS prior year}}{\text{EPS prior year}}$$

$$\text{Price--earnings ratio} = \frac{\text{Market price per share}}{\text{Earnings per share}}$$

$$\text{Dividend yield} = \frac{\text{Dividend per share}}{\text{Market price per share}}$$

$$\text{Dividend payout ratio} = \frac{\text{Dividend per share}}{\text{Earnings per share}}$$

Dividend Payout Ratio

The dividend payout ratio is the ratio of dividends per share to earnings per share. For Coca-Cola Company, the payout ratio in 1994 was 28 percent ($0.56/$1.98); in 1993, the ratio was 35 percent ($0.58/$1.67). Again, companies with high growth rates usually have relatively low dividend yields and payout ratios because they invest cash instead of paying dividends.

Most companies want a stable dividend payment pattern, as opposed to dividends that fluctuate with earnings. For this reason, the dividend amount, and not the payout ratio, is the principal consideration of dividend policy.

Exhibit 21–2 summarizes the ratios discussed in this chapter.

Index